TRUTH-TELLING

HENRY REYNOLDS is one of Australia's most recognised historians. He grew up in Hobart and was educated at Hobart High School and the University of Tasmania. In 1965, he accepted a lectureship at James Cook University in Townsville, which sparked an interest in the history of relations between settlers and Aboriginal people. In 2000, he took up a professorial fellowship at the University of Tasmania. His pioneering work has changed the way we see the intertwining of black and white history in Australia. His books with NewSouth include *The Other Side of the Frontier* (reissue); *What's Wrong with Anzac?* (as co-author); *Forgotten War*, which won the Victorian Premier's Literary Prize; *Unnecessary Wars*; and most recently *This Whispering in Our Hearts Revisited*.

'Our goal of an honourable place in the nation for Aboriginal and Torres Strait Islander people owes much to Henry Reynolds. He contributed his profound historical scholarship on the denial of sovereignty to Indigenous people in Australia when we were still trying to get a seat at the table in the United Nations. He has been cited in key documents since and his work informed the outcomes in Koiki Mabo's challenge to the High Court in *Mabo (No 2)*. His imprint is also evident in the Uluru Statement from the Heart. This book is essential reading for everyone involved in recognising our place in the nation.'

Marcia Langton

'Henry Reynolds once again exposes some of the horrible truths regarding our shared past. Laying an important foundation for truth-telling and treaty-making, *Truth-Telling* casts aside the lie of *terra nullius* that continues to have disastrous and ongoing consequences for Aboriginal peoples, and for the contemporary Australian nation. This book will allow Australians to build a better, more truthful, Australia.'

Mick Dodson

'With passion, readability, and scrupulous scholarship, Henry Reynolds lays out the big-picture context of the Uluru Statement from the Heart and why it's fundamental to our future Australia. Essential reading to understand the past and see the path forward.'

Kate Grenville

'This is the book we've been waiting for. The historian who pioneered a revolution in Aboriginal history helps us to understand the full majesty and historical depth of the Uluru Statement from the Heart. In doing so, he exposes the denial at the heart of Australia's foundation. Henry Reynolds writes with luminous clarity, piercing insight and moral power. *Truth-Telling* is a gift to his nation from one of our greatest historians, a brilliant encapsulation of a lifetime's scholarship.'

Tom Griffiths

'An eloquent and powerful distillation of a lifetime's work. Ranging across a vast terrain of scholarship as few other historians can – legal and political history, war and memory, and the brutal, chequered history of Australia's frontier – Henry Reynolds re-examines the traditional doctrine of sovereignty in light of the Uluru Statement from the Heart. How did the sovereignty of First Nations people survive the invasion? Is it possible for First Nations' sovereignty to "coexist with the sovereignty of the Crown"? With trademark clarity and intellectual rigour, Reynolds has given us a political call to arms; a book that explains like no other why Truth-Telling is so urgently needed in Australia.'

Mark McKenna

TRUTH-TELLING

HISTORY, SOVEREIGNTY
AND THE ULURU STATEMENT

HENRY REYNOLDS

NEWSOUTH

Warning: Aboriginal and Torres Strait Islander people should be aware that this book contains words and descriptions written by non-Indigenous people in the past that may be confronting and would be considered inappropriate today. It also contains the names of deceased Indigenous people and graphic descriptions of historical events that may be disturbing to some readers.

A NewSouth book

Published by
NewSouth Publishing
University of New South Wales Press Ltd
University of New South Wales
Sydney NSW 2052
AUSTRALIA
newsouthpublishing.com

© Henry Reynolds 2021
First published 2021

10 9 8 7 6 5 4 3 2 1

A catalogue record for this book is available from the National Library of Australia

ISBN: 9781742236940 (paperback)
          9781742245119 (ebook)
          9781742249636 (ePDF)

Design Josephine Pajor-Markus
Cover design Peter Long
Cover image The Landing of Captain Cook at Botany Bay 1770, Australia,
     1930 / Copyright Percy Trompf Artistic Trust, courtesy Josef Lebovic
     Gallery, Sydney
Printer Griffin Press

All reasonable efforts were taken to obtain permission to use copyright material reproduced in this book, but in some cases copyright could not be traced. The author welcomes information in this regard.

This book is printed on paper using fibre supplied from plantation or sustainably managed forests.

CONTENTS

THE ULURU STATEMENT FROM THE HEART

We, gathered at the 2017 National Constitutional Convention, coming from all points of the southern sky, make this statement from the heart:

Our Aboriginal and Torres Strait Islander tribes were the first sovereign Nations of the Australian continent and its adjacent islands, and possessed it under our own laws and customs. This our ancestors did, according to the reckoning of our culture, from the Creation, according to the common law from 'time immemorial', and according to science more than 60,000 years ago.

This sovereignty is a spiritual notion: the ancestral tie between the land, or 'mother nature', and the Aboriginal and Torres Strait Islander peoples who were born therefrom, remain attached thereto, and must one day return thither to be united with our ancestors. This link is the basis of the ownership of the soil, or better, of sovereignty. It has never been ceded or extinguished, and co-exists with the sovereignty of the Crown.

How could it be otherwise? That peoples possessed a land for sixty millennia and this sacred link disappears from world history in merely the last two hundred years?

With substantive constitutional change and structural

reform, we believe this ancient sovereignty can shine through as a fuller expression of Australia's nationhood.

Proportionally, we are the most incarcerated people on the planet. We are not an innately criminal people. Our children are aliened from their families at unprecedented rates. This cannot be because we have no love for them. And our youth languish in detention in obscene numbers. They should be our hope for the future.

These dimensions of our crisis tell plainly the structural nature of our problem. *This is the torment of our powerlessness*.

We seek constitutional reforms to empower our people and take a *rightful place* in our own country. When we have power over our destiny our children will flourish. They will walk in two worlds and their culture will be a gift to their country.

We call for the establishment of a First Nations Voice enshrined in the Constitution.

Makarrata is the culmination of our agenda: *the coming together after a struggle*. It captures our aspirations for a fair and truthful relationship with the people of Australia and a better future for our children based on justice and self-determination.

We seek a Makarrata Commission to supervise a process of agreement-making between governments and First Nations and truth-telling about our history.

In 1967 we were counted, in 2017 we seek to be heard. We leave base camp and start our trek across this vast country. We invite you to walk with us in a movement of the Australian people for a better future.[1]

INTRODUCTION:
HEARING THE STATEMENT
FROM THE HEART

I first became involved in the politics of race over fifty years ago. It was in 1967, at the time of the referendum to amend the Constitution. Two small changes were being proposed. One made it possible for the first time to count Indigenous Australians in the national census. The other gave the federal government power to become engaged in Aboriginal affairs, hitherto a state government preserve. But for the electorate at large it represented a chance to welcome Indigenous Australians into the political community. And perhaps, even more significantly, it permitted the federal government to take the leading role in both developing and funding new Indigenous policies. It was one of the milestones on the long road that slowly wound its way away from white Australia's colonial and racist past. There have been other milestones on the journey. There was the bark petition sent by the Yirrkala people of Arnhem Land's Gove Peninsula in 1963 attempting to overturn the decision to excise land from the Aboriginal Reserve to facilitate bauxite mining. In 1988, then prime minister Bob Hawke signed the Barunga Statement foreshadowing negotiations to precede the signing of a treaty. His successor, Paul Keating, delivered his Redfern Speech in December 1992 calling for recognition that indeed white Australia had a black history, declaring 'that it was we who did the dispossessing. We took the traditional lands and smashed the traditional way of life. We brought the diseases. The alcohol. We committed the murders. We took the children from their mothers.'[1] In 2008 the newly elected prime minister Kevin Rudd delivered a formal apology to the Stolen Generations.

In May 2017 the nation was presented with what has come to be known as the Statement from the Heart, drawn up after a meeting at Uluru of 250 delegates 'coming from all points of the southern sky'. The statement was the culmination of a process that followed the appointment of a sixteen-member Referendum Council in December 2015. Council members gathered evidence from over a thousand participants meeting at twelve locations around the country. There was not universal Indigenous support for the statement, but it was undoubtedly the most widely canvassed document that has ever been addressed to the wider community by representatives of the First Nations. It was also a masterpiece of forensic advocacy – succinct, with scarcely a wasted word, utilitarian where necessary, elegant, even poetic in places. It is a document that will endure. But its lasting political impact is yet to be determined.

The proposal that attracted most discussion was the call for the establishment of an institution to provide for a permanent Indigenous 'voice to parliament'. It was dismissed with peremptory expedition by then prime minister Malcolm Turnbull, who declared that it would become an unacceptable third chamber of parliament. Other suggestions in the document have so far escaped critical attention, but their long-term significance is likely to be considerable, presenting a feisty challenge to both Australian jurisprudence and the nation's perception of its history.

The delegates at Uluru called for the establishment of a Makarrata Commission to supervise a process of both agreement-making and truth-telling in our history. Makarrata is a Yolngu word describing a process of conflict resolution, peacemaking and justice. It would represent the first official and adequately funded body to examine the fraught history of relations between the First Nations and the European invaders. It would have to tackle questions that have been deeply controversial and much contested during the last two generations, ones that have been central to the culture wars still being fought out in parliaments, the media and the nation's school rooms. On the other hand, it would bring Australia into line with the many countries that, while dealing with troubled histories, have over the last thirty years or so established truth commissions. The South African Truth and Reconciliation Commission is probably the best known of these, but they were also established in South and Central America and in Eastern Europe. They provided venues for victims to be heard, and for atrocities to be documented in such a way that they will never be forgotten.

So while the Statement from the Heart urges Australia to come to terms with a radical new version of the nation's history, it throws up an even more challenging interpretation of the law and in particular our understanding of the imposing question of sovereignty. A passage of great eloquence declares that the Aboriginal and Torres Strait Islander peoples were the first sovereign nations of the Australian continent and possessed it under their own laws and customs:

> It has never been ceded or extinguished, and co-exists with the sovereignty of the Crown.
> How could it be otherwise? That peoples possessed a land for sixty millennia and this sacred link disappears from world history in merely the last two hundred years?
> … we believe this ancient sovereignty can shine through as a fuller expression of Australia's nationhood.[2]

We have here a series of assertions that have the rhetorical power of compacted common sense. But common sense is not the same thing as the common law. The idea that First Nations' sovereignty survived the invasion collides with the fundamental premises on which law in Australia was based from the first hours of colonisation. For good or ill, they remain undisturbed, buried deep in the legal foundations of the state.

The Statement, then, contains a challenge to legal doctrine more unsettling than the jurisprudential revolution ushered in by the High Court's *Mabo* judgment in 1992 and the *Wik* judgment four years later. Our first task in this book then is to re-examine the traditional doctrine of sovereignty, from the appearance of James Cook on the east coast of Australia in 1770 and the arrival of the First Fleet in Sydney Harbour eighteen years later, and bring it forward until 1992, when despite themselves the High Court judges in the *Mabo* case changed property law forever and intimated that the traditional doctrine relating to sovereignty might eventually have to change as well. Is it possible that the sovereignty of the First Nations has survived? Was it ever extinguished? Can it coexist with the sovereignty of the Crown? And what of truth-telling? Is there an appetite for it in contemporary Australia? Or is the need for comforting national stories too compelling? Are home truths just too difficult to accept?

These questions have interested me ever since I arrived in Townsville from Tasmania in 1965 to begin a teaching career at the new university college, which became James Cook University in 1970. I was asked to teach Australian history, which I knew very little about. I knew even less of the fraught relations between white Australians and the Aboriginal and Torres Strait Islander peoples. And it was a time of rapid change. Torres Strait Islanders had only been allowed to live on the Australian mainland for a few years, after having worked on rebuilding the Townsville–Mount Isa railway line. By 1966, many young men had brought wives and family members to live in Townsville and Cairns. At the same time there was what can only be called a reurbanisation of Aboriginal communities. Families were being allowed for the first time to leave hitherto closed reserves and missions. Others were being encouraged to walk away from pastoral stations in the vast hinterland as demands for equal pay grew louder.

The 1967 referendum marked the beginning of a new era in community relations. In Townsville the tensions accompanying rapid and radical social change were apparent every day and were, as a result, inescapable. And much of what one could see and hear was shocking. Old white Australia was resisting loudly and often violently. It was all totally new to me and in many ways unexpected. I was seeing aspects of Australia that I had known nothing about.

The students in my small classes knew that race was a question of pressing importance. Many of them had come from small towns, from pastoral stations or from Aboriginal missions where their parents taught. So how was I to bring these themes into my teaching? It was still in the era of what the anthropologist Bill Stanner called, in his 1968 Boyer Lectures, 'the great Australian silence'.[3] The textbook set for my course scarcely mentioned Aboriginal people. They did not even have an entry in the index. There were very few relevant books in the small university library. So I began, tentatively at first, to research Queensland history and then widen out my exploration to embrace the whole country. And at the same time I started some rudimentary exploration of oral history among the Aboriginal and Torres Strait Islander community, working with my friends Eddie Mabo and Noel Loos. For the first time I had the chance to see, vicariously, Australian history from the other side of the frontier. And having done so I could never again see our national story as one of triumphant progress and peaceful pioneering. It was not heroic, I came to realise, but tragic. I began to write a different sort of history, which was controversial and, for many people, deeply challenging. I became a leading practitioner of what was to be given the pejorative title 'black-armband' history.

My original focus was on the history of the shifting frontier where resident bands confronted the intruding white men. The accompanying violence was ubiquitous and therefore inescapable. But other themes emerged. The land rights crusade thrust legal questions to the front of both the political and the historical stages. It was a subject I knew little about, an ignorance remedied by many weeks of intense study in the practitioners' Library in the High Court in Canberra. And examination of land law led on to the related question of sovereignty. It became progressively clear that to bring the First Nations back into Australian history meant to challenge the hitherto imposing edifice of both the nation and the state. They could not be housed in a lean-to at the back of the building. The whole floor plan had to be redesigned.

Research, politics and law came together in a series of fateful meetings with Eddie Mabo and Noel Loos in my office in James Cook University. We told Eddie that his ancestors' land had been expropriated a hundred years before when, in 1879, the Queensland colonial government had annexed the Murray Islands. He was astonished, horrified and outraged. There was the extraordinary injustice to begin with, but also the grotesque imperial overreach permitted and sanctioned by the law. So, as far as Eddie was concerned, Queensland's claim of sovereignty was as dubious as the expropriation of his land. Had he lived he would have pursued that question with equal vigour and would likely have been one of the signatories of the Uluru Statement from the Heart.

I learnt so much from conversations with First Nations' friends and acquaintances all over Australia, but particularly in and around Townsville. But of equal importance have been the innumerable discussions I have had over many years in many parts of Australia with students, audiences in halls and churches, and attendees of conferences and literary festivals.

I have had many conversations with perfect strangers and have listened in to relevant discussions in which others were engaged. People were frequently supportive of my project, but not always so. I have been accused of disloyalty, of irresponsible troublemaking and of hating my country. During the Cold War, I was often denounced as a communist. More commonly I was called a ratbag. I quickly came to realise how difficult these questions were, particularly for older Australians who had grown up when a much more benign version of Australian history was taught in schools and was woven through our cultural life. Despite what many people thought, I was aware that 'black-armband' history was deeply disturbing, and I understood those many people who took the view that a troubled history was best forgotten, that it was preferable to look to the future and not to dwell on the past. But it was always hard to equate those sentiments with that most revered phrase in Australian history, 'Lest We Forget'.

Australians are sensitive about their past and most people have strong views about First Nations people. It is a subject about which almost everyone is willing to express an opinion, no matter how poorly informed. Certainly, the last twenty or so years have seen a remarkable growth of historical awareness and a far more realistic understanding of the whole process of colonisation. There is now a better chance than at any time in the recent past to initiate a process of truth-telling. But not everyone will be happy with the process, and opposition may make it hard to establish bipartisan support for the Makarrata as proposed by those many delegates at Uluru who had come 'from all points of the southern sky'.

My own individual contribution to our national truth-telling will begin with the arrival of the British when, in 1770, James Cook's *Endeavour* sailed along the east coast and then in January 1788, when the First Fleet arrived at Botany Bay before moving a few days later to the more promising site on Sydney Harbour.

PART I

THE FIRST
SOVEREIGN
NATIONS

I

TAKING POSSESSION

The *Endeavour* arrived on the south coast of Australia at Point Hicks, in Gippsland Victoria, on 20 April 1770, having earlier circumnavigated New Zealand. Cook turned north and anchored for a week in Botany Bay in late April and early May. He then resumed his run up the east coast, naming over a hundred prominent features and drawing up charts along the way. After taking forced refuge in the Endeavour River for seven weeks, the voyage continued, and by the third week in August the repaired ship was anchored beside a small island a few miles off the north-west coast of Cape York over 3000 kilometres from their Australian starting point. Seeking a safe passage westward 'into the India sea', Cook took a party onto the island and walked to the top of a small hill. He then performed a simple ceremony, the consequences of which have echoed down the generations.

Having concluded with confidence that no European had ever seen the continent's east coast he hoisted the English colours and in the evening light took possession of the country in His Majesty's name, together with all the bays, harbours, rivers and islands situated upon the coast. The party standing under the flag fired three volleys of small arms, which were answered from the ship. As the echoes of the gunfire faded away, Cook and his shipmates joined together in a chorus of three cheers. The unremarkable location was then named 'Possession Island'.

Cook's audacious claim has, not surprisingly, been seen as one of the defining moments in the history of Australian colonisation. But its true significance is still a matter of sharp controversy. The conventional view is that we should take Cook's actions at face value and, whether or not they meet contemporary expectations, accept the fact that Britain acquired sovereignty over the whole of eastern Australia at that climactic moment off the coast of Cape York. It's an interpretation that has obvious attractions. It meant that the contentious question of sovereignty was resolved once and for all even before the arrival eighteen years later of the First Fleet. And it was all done without serious conflict or bloodshed. Was there ever, anywhere, an easier acquisition? Cook himself could be admired as a great navigator and admirable personality who had, as a consequence of his 'discovery', earned for Britain the title over the 'Great South Land'.

But there is much wrong with this interpretation. The faults are numerous and various. They arise not from the judgments of our contemporaries but from the law and the morality of Cook's own time. There is, to begin with, the matter of discovery. Was it possible to discover an already peopled land? The great 17th-century Dutch jurist Hugo Grotius had a very clear view of the matter, writing that 'Equally shameless is it to claim for oneself by right of discovery what is held by another, even though the occupant may be wicked, may hold wrong views about God, or may be dull of wit. For discovery applies to those things which belong to no one.'[1] Clearly Cook and the whole ship's company knew that the entire long coastline was occupied by the Aboriginal people, even if their actual contact with them was limited.

This brings us to an even more contested question. Did Cook's claim of possession dispossess the resident Indigenous nations? Many commentators have believed that it did. Cook's secret instructions of 30 July 1768 are frequently referred to. They included the following injunction: 'You are also with the consent of the Natives to take Possession of Convenient Situations in the name of the King of Great Britain; or, if you find the Country uninhabited take Possession for His Majesty by setting up Proper Marks and Inscriptions, as first discoverers and possessors.'[2]

The two parts of these instructions are quite different. Many commentators have argued that Cook wilfully disobeyed the injunction to gain the consent of the natives. But he nowhere attempted to take possession of convenient situations with an eye on future settlement, which was not being considered at the time. But the second part of the instructions opens up an array of problems. Did Cook wilfully behave as though eastern Australia was uninhabited when he knew full well that it wasn't? If so, it was a serious dereliction of duty with little basis in either international law at the time or widely accepted morality. The most pertinent illustration of contemporary standards can be found in the material presented to him by James Douglas, the 14th Earl of Morton, on behalf of the Royal Society, which had sponsored the voyage into the southern seas. Writing about the Indigenous people that the voyagers would encounter, Morton observed that they should be seen as 'the natural, and in the strictest sense of the word, the legal possessors of the several Regions they inhabit' and that even conquest of 'such a people can give no just title'.[3]

But much of the discussion relating to Cook's claim of possession proceeds without a clear understanding about what such assertions meant at the time. By the late 18th century, the purpose of claims based on 'discovery' were well understood, and many of the European maritime powers employed them as a means to stake out spheres of influence in other parts of the world and thereby seek to avoid perpetual conflict. Cook's claim was directed at Britain's European rivals, not at the First Nations living along the east coast. There is an intimation of this proposition in the fact that he referred to the bays, harbours and rivers while making no mention as to how far inland the claim reached. The American jurists, not surprisingly, provided the clearest definition of how a claim based on 'discovery' related to Indigenous peoples. Chief Justice John Marshall of the American Supreme Court determined in a famous case, *Worcester v Georgia*, in 1832 that such claims 'asserted a title against Europeans only and were considered as blank pages so far as the rights of the natives were concerned'.[4] In his study *Commentaries on the Constitution of the United States*, Marshall's colleague Joseph Story observed that the accepted rule was that discovery might 'properly govern all the nations, which recognized its obligation; but it could have no authority over the aborigines of America, whether gathered into civilized communities, or scattered in hunting tribes over the wilderness'.[5]

The leading 20th-century authority on the subject, MF Lindley, observed in his authoritative study, *The Acquisition and Government of Backward Territory in International Law*, that:

> discovery ... was adopted to regulate the competition between European Powers themselves, and it had no bearing upon the relations between those powers and the natives. What the discoverer's State gained was the right, as against other European Powers, to take steps which were appropriate to the acquisition of the territory in question. What those steps were would depend on whether there was already a native population in possession of the territory ...[6]

Cook's ceremony on Possession Island did not therefore amount to all that much. On its own it would have mattered no more than Tasman's claim of ownership over Tasmania dating back to 1642, or for that matter the claim over Western Australia made at Shark Bay by a French expedition in 1772. To spring to life it had to be followed up by a permanent occupation of the kind that took place eighteen years later. Grotius remarked that a claim based on discovery could be the basis for an assertion of sovereignty 'only when it is accompanied by actual possession'.[7] In his 1741 book *A Methodical System of Universal Law*, JG Heineccius observed that an individual or a nation, who only 'seized a thing with his eyes, but does not take hold of it, cannot be said to occupy'.[8]

So Cook's famous voyage along almost the whole length of Australia's east coast bestowed many names on geographical features observed from the quarterdeck that remain on the map to this day. But the crew had very limited contact with the resident Aboriginal peoples. And his claim of possession had no effect on Indigenous land ownership or on their sovereignty. The arrival of the First Fleet in January 1788 was a much more serious challenge and must be examined now.

Arthur Phillip received his commissions from the King on 12 October 1786 and 2 April the following year. Significantly, they differed greatly from the ones issued to Cook in 1768 before he sailed for the Pacific. Missing was the instruction to 'take possession of convenient situations with the consent of the natives'. The absence requires some explaining. It was standard practice to refer to the need to obtain the informed consent of resident nations, both before and after 1788. In 1776, when Cook was preparing for another voyage into the Pacific, he was once again instructed to take possession of convenient locations 'with the consent of the Natives'.[9] In 1785 the British government was considering the possibility of establishing a penal settlement on the West African coast at Das Voltas Bay, now Lüderitz Bay in modern-day Namibia. The House of Commons Committee on Transportation reported that it was 'highly probable that the Natives would, without Resistance, acquiesce in Ceding as much Land as may be necessary, for a stipulated Rent'. The committee added that all the 'Portuguese and Dutch Possessions on that Coast have been so acquired'.[10] In 1790 Britain affirmed the same principles when engaged in diplomatic conflict with Spain about Nootka Sound on the north-west coast of America, now in Canada. The British negotiators insisted that the Spanish accept, as a principle, the right to establish any settlement 'as English subjects ... should form with the consent of the natives of the country not previously occupied by any European nation'. The British had their way and the principle was embodied in the resulting Anglo-Spanish Convention of October 1790.[11]

Why was Phillip not instructed to seek the 'consent of the natives' at a location convenient for a penal settlement? We don't have enough evidence to be certain about the discussions that preceded the decision to send the First Fleet to the far end of the world. It was a momentous one for officials to make when none of them had any first-hand knowledge about Australia. They paid particular attention to two men who had been with Cook, the aristocrat president of the Royal Society, Joseph Banks, and the American loyalist James Matra, who presented a paper to the government entitled 'A proposal for establishing a settlement in New South Wales' in August 1783. Matra observed that many new countries had been found 'which know no sovereign' and which held out the 'most enticing allurements to European adventurers'. None was more inviting than New South Wales because:

In this immense tract of more than 2,000 miles there was every variety of soil, and great parts of it were extremely fertile, peopled only by a few black inhabitants, who, in the rudest state of society, knew no other arts than such as were necessary to their mere animal existence, and which was almost entirely sustained by catching fish.[12]

Matra's enthusiasm for the allurements was probably not as persuasive as the views of Banks, who also insisted that eastern Australia was 'thinly inhabited even to admiration'.[13] The expedition had seen no large gatherings, and the evidence provided by abandoned camp sites 'convinced us of the smallness of their parties'. Expedition members had been ashore fourteen times but they were all on the seashore or offshore islands. They knew nothing about the vast inland, Banks admitting that what it might produce 'is to us totally unknown'. Nevertheless he made a truly portentous assumption arguing that 'we may have liberty to conjecture that [it is] totally uninhabited'. Without access to the sea there was nothing that could sustain life. These views were clearly persuasive and found their way into books written about Australia before the First Fleet had arrived at its destination. The continent was described as the 'solitary haunt of a few miserable savages'; the population was very small in proportion to its extent and there was 'reason to believe' that the interior was 'either wholly desolate, or at least still more thinly inhabited than the places which have been visited'.[14]

Banks provided pivotal evidence to the Commons Committee on Transportation in May 1785. Was the coast of New South Wales much inhabited, they asked, to which the great man observed that there were very few inhabitants and the ship's crew 'never saw more than thirty or forty together'. And while they seemed 'inclined to Hostilities they did not appear at all to be feared'. They were armed with spears but none of them seen at Botany Bay were considered at all formidable. The committee inquired: 'Do you apprehend, in Case it was resolved to send convicts there, any District of the Country might be obtained by Cession or purchase?' Both the question and the following exchange provide a key to understanding the instructions prepared for Phillip in October the following year. Banks declared that 'There was no probability while we were there of obtaining anything either by Cession or Purchase as there was nothing we could offer that they would take except provisions. Those we wanted ourselves.'

The committee then asked: 'Have you any idea of the nature of the Government under which they lived?' and Banks responded: 'None whatever nor of their language.' An even more pertinent question followed: 'Do you think that 500 men being put on shore there would meet with that Obstruction from the Natives which might prevent them settling there?' Banks replied emphatically: 'Certainly not – from the experience I have had of the Natives of another part of the same Coast I am inclined to believe they would speedily abandon the country to the newcomers.'[15]

The persuasive power of the testimony of Matra and Banks can be seen in the reaction of Arthur Phillip when he sent his early reports from Sydney back to the imperial government. Things in New South Wales were not the way that he had been led to expect. There were far more Aboriginal people to start with. The country was not thinly inhabited. In July 1788 Phillip explained in two letters that 'the natives are far more numerous than they were supposed to be'. He estimated that there could 'not be less than fifteen hundred' in the broad area around Sydney Cove.[16] And even more to the point the inhabitants showed no intention of abandoning the country.

Phillip was not the only member of the expedition who found their original preconceptions disrupted by colonial reality. Captain Watkin Tench noted that even at the mouth of the harbour they 'had reason to conclude the country more populous than Mr Cook had thought it'.[17] Captain John Hunter agreed, finding the Aboriginal people around the harbour 'very numerous', a situation he was 'a little surprized to find, after what had been said of them in the voyage of the *Endeavour*'.[18] The fundamental reassessment was being reported back in England by 1789 in *An Authentic and Interesting Narrative of the Late Expedition to Botany Bay*. The anonymous author noted that Cook had only seen a few Aboriginal people and had 'therefore concluded that the country was thinly inhabited [but] in this manner he was much mistaken, as frequently tribes of three or four hundred came down together'.[19]

But Phillip seemed even more troubled by the fact that it increasingly looked as though the interior was not uninhabited as Banks had supposed. In an early letter back to London he reported that in a short journey into the hinterland he 'was surprised to find temporary huts made by the natives far inland'. He provided an explanation that would, for the moment, help preserve the orthodox view the expedition had brought with it from London, remarking: 'I believe their numbers in the woods must be very small. Whether they live in the woods by choice, or are driven from the society of those who inhabit the sea-coast, or whether they travel to a distant part of the country, I can form no judgment at present.'[20]

He explained that members of his reconnaissance party had poked around in old fireplaces looking for evidence that would prove the residents had been eating fish brought back from the coast. Phillip explained: 'We saw many places where the natives had made fires, but at one place only were any oyster and mussel shells, and then not more than half a dozen, and no fish bones, so that when they go inland they certainly do not carry fish to support them.'[21] Two months later the evidence was even more troubling. The small community clustered near the harbour had seen smoke on the Blue Mountains 'fifty miles inland'. Phillip declared that as soon as the spring weather permitted he intended going up to the mountains and endeavour to explain 'what is at present a mystery to me, how people who have not the least idea of cultivation can maintain themselves in the interior parts of this country'.[22]

Every party that subsequently ventured inland returned with mounting evidence that the idea the interior was uninhabited was seriously awry. In April 1791, Tench met a man who told him that his people 'depended but very little on fish' and that their principal support came from small animals and yams, which they 'dug out of the earth'.[23] By 1802, Francis Barrallier, an engineer and explorer, was able to compile a list of the wide varieties of food used by the inland bands, who also 'appeared to be very good hunters'.[24]

Phillip's anguish about the inland Aborigines is understandable, because much of the rationale for major provisions in his official instructions depended on the twin ideas of a coastal littoral 'thinly inhabited even to admiration' and an unpeopled hinterland, literally a *terra nullius*. These two tragic misconceptions help explain why British behaviour was so exceptional. They did not, in the manner of Cook's instructions, take possession of 'convenient locations on the coast'. Nor did they occupy 'as much land as was necessary' for the penal settlement as was proposed on the west coast of Africa in the same manner as both the Dutch and the Portuguese. They made the truly extraordinary claim of half the continent. They pushed Cook's claim southwards to include Tasmania, which had been earlier 'discovered' by first the Dutch and then the French and was still thought to be attached to the mainland. While Cook had not suggested any landward extension from the coast, Phillip's commission claimed all the territory westward to 135 degrees of longitude, a line extending right down through the middle of what became South Australia and the Northern Territory.

It was truly an astonishing assertion of sovereignty that had almost no credibility in international law. The 20th-century expert on British Commonwealth law Sir Kenneth Roberts-Wray thought that it was 'indeed startling, and, indeed incredible'.[25] The law relating to territorial claims following colonisation was, of necessity, closely considered by European international jurists. It all depended on the area actually occupied by agents of the imperial power. In the case of Australia that meant, up until the colonisation of Tasmania in 1803–04, the area within a short distance of Sydney. The established rule was that the occupying power could make a legitimate claim over all the land drained by the rivers whose mouths were actually in its possession. The standard understanding was outlined by WE Hall in his 1889 *A Treatise on International Law*. What, he asked, was involved in the occupation of a given portion of shore? He answered in some detail:

It may be regarded as settled usage that the interior limit shall not extend further than the crest of the watershed; but the lateral frontiers are less certain. It is generally admitted that occupation of the coast carries with it the right to the whole territory drained by the rivers which empty their waters within its line; but the admission of this right is perhaps accompanied by the tacit reservation that the extent of coast must bear some reasonable proportion to the territory which is claimed in virtue of possession. It has been maintained, but it can hardly be conceded, that the whole of a large river basin is so attendant upon the land in the immediate neighbourhood of its outlet that property in it is acquired by merely holding a fort or settlement at the mouth of the river without also holding lands to any distance on either side.[26]

So even at the high tide of European imperialism there were constraints on the legitimacy of the right to annex vast areas of land and to make a supportable claim of sovereignty. There had to be some reasonable relationship between actual occupation on the ground and the reach of claimed territory. The establishment of the small penal colony on Sydney Harbour gave absolutely no legitimacy to the British claim to half a continent, home to many Indigenous nations, which had occupied their homelands for hundreds of generations. The fact that the claim was drawn up in Britain before the First Fleet had set sail accentuates what can fairly be called the absurdity embedded in the instructions handed to Phillip in October 1786 and formally read by him on the shore of

Sydney Cove on 7 February 1788. They may have seemed reasonable in London if the relevant officials accepted Banks's assertion that most of the great landmass was uninhabited and Matra's argument that New South Wales was home to a few savages living in the rudest state of society. In that case Britain could assert that no one exercised sovereignty and that what the Crown acquired was an original rather than a derived sovereignty. How much more realistic it would have been if Phillip's party had claimed to be in control of an area sufficient for the establishment of the penal settlement and then sought out the appropriate way to relate to the resident bands and even considered what was accepted international practice. By at least 1800 the more enlightened colonists, men like Watkin Tench, David Collins and Francis Barrallier, had developed considerable understanding of the Indigenous way of life, certainly sufficient to negotiate local treaties.

So while geographical and ethnographic understanding went one way, the law continued to follow the trajectory marked out in Britain in 1786. The gap between law and reality, law and colonial experience, grew progressively wider. Australian jurisprudence retreated further from the real world and consequently became more deeply entangled in injustice. The myth of the unpeopled land was too convenient to discard, and abandoning it would have demanded radical changes in law and politics and the whole way the colonisation of Australia was understood. So in 1819, the Crown law officers determined that New South Wales had been annexed as a result of being 'desert and uninhabited'.[27] The *South Australia Act* of 1834 referred to the land of the planned colony as being 'waste and unoccupied'.[28] In a judgment of 1849, the chief justice of New South Wales referred to the 'circumstances of newly discovered and unpeopled territories'.[29] The idea was sanctified and put beyond the reach of Australian courts by the British Privy Council in 1889. In the case of *Cooper v Stuart*, the court declared that in 1788 Australia had consisted of a 'tract of territory practically unoccupied without settled inhabitants'.[30] So after a hundred years of colonisation, the misconceptions held by imperial officials in 1786 trumped everything that had been learned at the antipodes. What is even more extraordinary, the case was considered to be binding on Australian Courts until the spell was finally broken by Justice Lionel Murphy in the High Court in 1975.[31]

Not that the question of sovereignty has been resolved. The idea of the empty land still overshadows our institutional thinking. There has been no official rejection of the way Britain claimed sovereignty over the whole continent in 1788, 1824 and 1829. It remains cemented into the foundations of the Australian state. How this can enhance a respect for the law in the 21st century is hard to discern. Why First Nations people should accept the fantasy that their sovereignty disappeared with the stroke of a pen long ago in a distant land has yet to be addressed. But there is still much to consider. Could the sovereignty of the First Nations have been recognised in European international law of the 18th and 19th centuries? What of the attempts to change the traditional outlook in the Australian colonies? Although the standard Australian view is that while British annexation was not something that would be countenanced today it was legally sound and morally acceptable at the time, with the intellectual backing of European international law. Attempts to undermine this venerable protective wall are dismissed with the patronising assessment that sentimental, well-meaning anachronism has no place in serious historical or judicial interpretation.

It is, then, not surprising that Indigenous Australians lack any confidence in the law developed by the European powers during the age of imperial expansion, believing that it would invariably be on the side of the big battalions. This is indeed often, but not always, the case, as the following examination of international law at the time of the colonisation of Australia will show.

2

THIS ANCIENT SOVEREIGNTY

The British claim of sovereignty over the eastern half of the continent was an audacious territorial appropriation based, as we have seen, on a number of key ideas: that the interior of the great landmass was very likely uninhabited; and that the tribes who lived on the coast had no permanent ties to territory, would abandon the land occupied by the Europeans, and were too primitive to have any political organisation. But colonial experience undermined all of these assumptions and, in retrospect, the rationale for the annexation.

The first to go, as we have seen, was the belief that there were very few people living on the land. A second one was that the bands moved across the land and did not effectively occupy it. This belief only prevailed for a short time. The members of the First Fleet quickly realised that the Aboriginal peoples of the Sydney area lived in tribal groups, that each group occupied a specific district with known boundaries, and that they took their name from the district and rarely moved outside it. John Hunter wrote in his journal a few months after the arrival:

We had reason to believe, that the natives associate in tribes of many families together, and it appeared now that they have one fixed residence, and the tribe takes its name from the place of their general residence: you may often visit the place where the tribe resides, without finding the whole society there; their time is so much occupied in search of food, that the different families take different routes; but, in case of any dispute with a neighbouring tribe, they can be soon assembled.[1]

The interlopers came to realise that tribal boundaries were of long standing. Coastal residents knew little about the hinterland. The Aboriginal guides who accompanied the earliest inland expeditions saw country that was as new to them as it was to their European travelling companions, who were fascinated by formal diplomatic protocols necessary when entering land belonging to other tribes. In April 1791, Watkin Tench was travelling inland with two local Aboriginal men he knew as Boladeree and Colbee when he witnessed the following exchange:

Colbee no longer hesitated, but gave them the signal of invitation, in a loud hollow cry. After some whooping, and shouting, on both sides, a man, with a lighted stick in his hand, advanced near enough to converse with us. The first words, which we could distinctly understand were, 'I am Colbee, of the tribe of Cad-i-gal.' The stranger replied, 'I am Ber-ee-wan, of the tribe of Boorooberongal'. Boladeree informed him also of his name, and that

we were white men and friends, who would give him
something to eat. Still he seemed irresolute. Colbee
therefore advanced to him, took him by the hand, and led
him to us. By the light of the moon, we were introduced
to this gentleman, all our names being repeated in form
by our two masters of the ceremonies, who said we were
Englishmen, and Bud-ye-ree [good], that we came from
the sea coast, and that we were travelling inland.[2]

Other Europeans travelling inland had similar experiences.[3]

Evidence crowded in upon the white men, which forced
them to discard the prejudices brought from Europe that
the Aboriginal inhabitants were nomadic people who could
easily move on and find other hunting grounds. Apart from
anything else, every exploring party that ventured out from
the small infant towns returned with information about ever
more Aboriginal tribes. There was no unpeopled land. Writing after considerable experience on the fringes of European
settlement, Edward Eyre observed

that no part of the country is so utterly worthless, as not
to have attractions sufficient occasionally to tempt the
wandering savage into its recesses. In the arid, barren
naked plains of the north, with not a shrub to shelter him
from the heat, not a stick to burn for his fire … the native
is found, and where, as far as I could ascertain, the whole
country around appeared equally devoid of either animal
or vegetable life.[4]

Of all the canards inherited from the voyage of the *Endeavour* the idea that there was nothing to eat in the inland was quickly discarded as evidence to the contrary mounted with every passing year. The Europeans came to realise just how extensive and varied were Aboriginal food sources, that almost everything edible was exploited at some time or other during a typical year. The missionary Francis Tuckfield observed that: 'Prior to our coming among them every forest ... every valley ... every plain and sheet of water furnished its number of repasts at the proper season.'[5] Eyre came to realise that the Aboriginal peoples were dependent on 'the intimate knowledge they have of every nook and corner of the country they inhabit'.[6] Fellow explorer and colonial governor George Grey appreciated that in their own country the local bands knew 'exactly what it produces, the proper time at which the several articles are in season, and the readiest means of procuring them'.[7]

The Aboriginal peoples' constant use of fire to manage their own territories was noted by travellers and settlers. It was hard to miss, given the ever present clouds of smoke. From the earliest years of settlement, travellers were intrigued by open areas of grassland scattered among the forests 'as if they had been cleared by manual labour'.[8] As early as 1790, thoughtful observers appreciated how fire was used to shape the landscape, John Hunter writing:

> They also, when in considerable numbers, set the country
> on fire for several miles extent; this, we have generally
> understood, is for the purpose of disturbing such animals

as may be within reach of the conflagration; and thereby they have an opportunity of killing many. We have also had much reason to believe, that those fires were intended to clear that part of the country through which they have frequent occasion to travel, of the brush and underwood, from which they, being naked, suffer very great inconvenience. The fires, which we very frequently saw, particularly in the summertime, account also for an appearance, which, when we arrived here, we were much perplexed to understand the cause of; this was that two-thirds of the trees in the woods were very much scorched with fire, some were burnt quite black, up to the very top: as to the cause of this appearance we differed much in our opinions; but it is now plain, that it has ever been occasioned by the fires, which the natives so frequently make ...[9]

Another feature of Aboriginal society that captured the attention of curious settlers was the extraordinary diversity of languages. As they travelled inland they quickly appreciated that after a few days' journey they often came across new bands speaking an unknown language. They were particularly struck by the fact that the Aboriginal guides who accompanied virtually all inland expeditions, official or private, soon passed beyond their linguistic range and they too were among people whose language was incomprehensible. The noted French explorer Louis de Freycinet had spent time in many different parts of the continent and had keenly studied the First Nations. Summing up his wide experience, he noted that despite the great size of the continent there was a great similarity of appearance, manners and possessions. But he wondered 'How, despite all these similarities, it is possible to explain the infinite diversity of languages that are encountered at almost every step?' He came to the conclusion that it 'obviously results from the tight closed circle that each group occupies' and the 'paucity of contact between groups'.[10]

But for settlers everywhere the most troubling fact about the behaviour of the First Nations was that they strongly contested the encroachment on their traditional lands. They stood their ground and resisted the invasion with every means available to them. And they characteristically fought to defend their own country and nowhere else. In doing so they affirmed their rights as proprietors, and in attempting to apply their customary law to the interlopers they also continued to exercise sovereignty over their own territory. Large numbers of them died in what was frequently, if not always, an uneven conflict. But even when terrorised into outward acquiescence, they did not normally desert their traditional places or concede that they had ceased to be theirs, even in those closely settled districts where they were soon outnumbered. And the same pattern was repeated all over the country from the late 18th to the early 20th century. It is without doubt one of the most significant aspects of Australian history. By their serial resistance, they proved beyond doubt that the many tribes were nations, albeit small ones, that could have been accorded that status in the law of the European powers.

First Nations' resistance in both New South Wales and Tasmania was not an instinctive reaction to invasion, a visceral drive for revenge or an upsurge of savagery. It was political violence, and understandable as such by perceptive Europeans. The warriors were patriots and saw themselves in that way. A young military officer, William Darling, who spent time with the exiled Tasmanians on the islands in Bass Strait observed that they 'considered themselves as engaged in a justifiable war against the invaders of their country'.[11] The missionary and so-called protector of Aborigines George Augustus Robinson spent even more time with the Tasmanian Aboriginal peoples out in the bush, and declared that 'they were staunch lovers of their country' who considered 'every injury they can inflict upon White Men as an Act of Duty and patriotism and however they may dread the punishment which our laws inflict on them – they consider the sufferers under those punishments as Martyrs in the cause of their country'.[12]

A correspondent wrote to the *Hobart Town Gazette* in 1824 arguing that the settlers 'ought to feel that we have invaded a domain from which our invasion has expelled those who were born, bred, and providentially supplied in it'.[13] A 'Border Settler' writing in *The Tasmanian* three years later observed that the papers were full of accounts of Aboriginal aggression but little attention was given to the other side of the story, or to a 'race of men, whose crime is that of repelling the invaders of their country'.[14] Another settler wrote to the government arguing than the Aboriginal people were no more deserving of censure than the colonists would be in similar circumstances if they decided to 'expel or extirpate an invading enemy who stripped them of their property; forcibly imposed strange laws and customs on them and wantonly robbed them of existence'. But those who kill us, he observed 'are execrated as murderers whilst those who kill for us are celebrated as patriots'.[15]

Frontier conflict was an inevitable consequence of the manner in which the British annexed Australia. It was not what had been expected when the First Fleet departed. Banks had, as we have seen, assured his contemporaries that the 'natives' would not fight for territory and anyway their weapons were not to be feared. Governor Phillip wrote, while still in England, that it would be 'a great point gained' if the expedition could proceed 'in this business without having any dispute with the natives'.[16] And he sought to avoid conflict in the first few months, emphasising his determination that 'nothing less than the most absolute necessity should ever make me fire upon them'.[17]

But the instruction given to Phillip to treat the natives with 'amity and kindness'[18] could not assuage their sense of outrage at the invasion and occupation of their homelands. There had not been any negotiation, let alone the drafting of a treaty. With both their sovereignty and their property rights disregarded, they had nothing they could negotiate with. They were, therefore, never consulted. Lieutenant William Bradley observed that the natives were 'well pleased with our people until they began clearing the Ground at which they were displeased and wanted them gone'.[19] Collins thought about the situation after the troops had fired on a party of Aboriginal people who were taking potatoes from a garden. It was, he wrote:

much to be regretted that any necessity existed for adopting these sanguinary punishments, and that we had not yet been able to reconcile the natives to the deprivation of those parts of this harbour which we occupied. While they entertained the idea of us having dispossessed them of their residences, they must always consider us as enemies; and upon this principle they made a point of attacking the white people whenever opportunity and safety concurred.[20]

Collins' observation was both perceptive and prescient. The logic it enfolded continued to unravel for more than a century, all over the continent.

Tench observed how Phillip and his officers grew tired of 'this state of petty warfare and endless uncertainty'.[21] There was a consequent rapid descent into what, by definition, was extrajudicial violence against people who were in theory British subjects 'within the King's peace'.[22] The tipping point came in December 1790, when the convict McEntire, known as the governor's gamekeeper, was speared near Botany Bay and brought back to the settlement mortally wounded. Phillip ordered Tench to lead a detachment of fifty marines to take punitive action. But neither the first nor a follow-up expedition was able to 'come up' with the local band. The significance of the failed forays was that, as Tench reported, his first instructions were to capture two men and bring them in and to kill ten others, who were to be decapitated and the heads brought back as trophies in the bags provided. At Tench's suggestion the punishment was moderated. He was to capture six tribesmen and bring them back. Two were to be hanged and four sent to Norfolk Island. If the capture could not be effected, six were to be shot and beheaded. It is important to remember that at this stage McEntire was still alive and his attacker, Pemulwuy, was known and identified, meaning he could potentially have been tried and likely convicted.

Tench recorded Phillip's explanation of what had induced him 'to adopt measures of such severity'. Seventeen of 'our people had either been killed or wounded by the natives', he declared, and against the tribe he knew as the Bid-ee-gal he was determined to 'strike a decisive blow, in order, at once to convince them of our superiority' and to 'infuse an universal terror, which might operate to prevent farther mischief'.[23] Hunter provided a similar report, observing that Phillip was convinced that 'nothing but a severe example, and fear of having all the tribes who resided near the settlement destroyed would have the desired effect'. Hunter feared 'that the innocent might suffer' but he hoped the punishments inflicted on a few would in the end 'be an act of mercy to numbers'.[24]

Conflict escalated as settlers moved out into the hinterland and particularly along the river flats of the Hawkesbury Valley. In 1795 the soldiers were dispatched with orders to 'destroy as many as they could meet with of the wood tribe; and, in the hope of striking terror, to erect gibbets in different places, whereon the bodies of all they might kill were to be hung'.[25] Governor Philip Gidley King reported to his superiors in London that in the fighting the Aboriginal peoples suffered disproportionately; indeed, there was 'an astonishing difference' in the casualties.[26] The general situation was unchanged when Governor Lachlan Macquarie arrived in the colony in 1809. Like his predecessors he began with good intentions, but Aboriginal resistance persisted and he decided on what became known as acts of decisive severity. In 1816 he explained to the Colonial Office that he intended to drive the troublesome tribes to a distance 'so as to strike them with Terror against committing similar Acts of Violence in future'. Six months later, while discussing the consequences of a succeeding punitive expedition, he admitted that while women and children may have died, the severity would 'eventually strike Terror amongst the surviving Tribes, and deter them from the further Commission of such Sanguinary Outrages and Barbarities'.[27]

When Macquarie wrote this letter, the British had been in New South Wales for thirty years. Nothing much had changed. Succeeding administrations had found themselves using terror to try to suppress what was clearly an ongoing Indigenous insurgency. The governors were driven to this contingency without pleasure. They would have almost certainly preferred a more humane resolution to their problems. But Aboriginal violence was a serious difficulty. They would all have faced the clamour of the small British community to act decisively to bring the conflict to an end. But the nature of Aboriginal society created endless frustration. It was almost impossible to find the warriors in the bush. They knew and were at home in their territory. The settlers had few maps. The military were of little use. The advance of detachments across country was always known well in advance. So if it was impossible to 'come up' with the insurgent bands, what else could be done?

In other places tribal enemies could be punished in a variety of ways. Their villages could be destroyed, domestic animals run off or killed, crops burnt, wells poisoned. None of these time-honoured tactics were available in Australia. And then there was the political organisation based on small, self-sufficient nations. So the terror the settlers talked about and practised could only be effective in a relatively small area. And while those nations close to the villages and farms were eventually forced into submission, often because they came to depend on the Europeans for food and young men and women were absorbed into the local workforce, then the process had to start all over again as the settlers moved further out into the hinterland. The 'pacification' of one nation may have had little effect on their neighbours, who had to decide for themselves how they would deal with the relentless arrival of ever more white people.

With the rapid increase of both free settler and convict arrivals in the early 1820s, conflict flared in both New South Wales and Tasmania. By then the failure of policies pursued since 1788 could not be overlooked, leading to a dramatic change of approach contained in instructions given to Ralph Darling on his appointment to the governorship of New South Wales in 1825. During his voyage to Sydney, he visited Hobart and gave the relevant dispatch to Governor George Arthur with instructions to put the new policy into operation. The Secretary of State for the Colonies, Lord Bathurst, instructed his two Australian governors on 'the manner, in which the Native Inhabitants' were 'to be treated when making hostile incursions for the purpose of Plunder'. They were to understand it to be their duty, 'when such disturbances cannot be prevented or allayed by less vigorous measures, to oppose force by force, and to repel such Aggressions in the same manner, as if they proceeded from subjects of any accredited State'.[28] Arthur shaped his policy in the manner proposed and read the instructions to gatherings of his key officials.

Although often overlooked in accounts of the period, Bathurst's instructions represented a dramatic change of direction. The Aboriginal nations on and beyond the fringes of settlement were no longer considered to be British subjects, but national enemies representing 'accredited' states. The word accredited was obviously carefully chosen and comes from the world of diplomacy, meaning 'to authorise as an envoy or ambassador'. The claim that British sovereignty reached out to the centre of the continent had been abandoned. It had been replaced with the far more realistic and defensible view that it existed only where effective uncontested occupation had been imposed. The insurgent Aboriginal nations were to be regarded as enemies and not rebels or, in the local parlance, bushrangers. When martial law was imposed in each of the colonies, the Aboriginal peoples were placed 'on the footing of open enemies of the King, in a state of actual warfare against him', in the words of Tasmania's solicitor-general and later chief justice of New South Wales Alfred Stephen.[29]

George Arthur himself constantly referred to the ongoing conflict as war and he was a career military officer, as were many of his officials. In his correspondence he referred to war on many occasions, and although the phrasing changed the meaning remained constant. It was, variously, 'lawless and cruel warfare', 'lawless warfare', 'our continued warfare', 'our unpleasant warfare', 'the warfare with the natives', 'this lamented and protracted warfare', 'the species of warfare ... which is of the most distressing nature' and 'a war of the most dreadful kind'. Aboriginal peoples who were captured or ceased fighting were treated as prisoners of war rather than criminals. When members of the white bushranging gangs were brought into Hobart they were chained and were taken to prison, rapidly tried and hanged. The last warrior band to come to a settlement marched along the same road carrying their spears and proceeded to Government House for a formal meeting with the governor. The House of Commons paper on the situation in the colony, published in 1831, was termed *Military Operations Lately Carried on against the Aboriginal Inhabitants of Van Diemen's Land*.[30]

The question of British sovereignty confronted the Colonial Office again when officials were dealing with the private colonising company that was planning a new settlement in South Australia. Half of the territory in question had been claimed in 1788, the balance in 1824. While considering how to define the limits of the new colony in 1835, the under-secretary, James Stephen, wrote to his minister Lord Glenelg: 'H.M. [His Majesty] is to fix the boundaries of the Province. How this is to be done in a Terra incognito I cannot imagine, nor how it can be done at all with any due regard to the rights of the present Proprietors of the Soil or rulers of the country.'[31] Both the man and the message were of great significance. Stephen was at the time the pre-eminent expert in colonial law. He had been an official legal adviser to the government since 1813, had joined the Colonial Office in 1825 and become under-secretary in 1836, a position he held until 1847. He was the most influential holder of the office in the 19th century.

What Stephen said was equally significant. In a memo to his minister we must assume he was speaking with high seriousness. The Crown, he clearly asserted, did not exercise sovereignty over the interior of Australia, nor did it have title to the land. Both belonged to the present proprietors and rulers of the country. The law as proclaimed by Arthur Phillip in January 1788 was little more than an ambit claim with no juristic substance. And the Aboriginal peoples had rights and above all were assumed to be there in occupation of their land. There was no *terra nullius*. What is possibly even more significant was that Stephen had adopted the conventional view about Australian settlement twelve years earlier, writing that New South Wales was acquired 'neither by conquest nor cession but by the mere occupation of a desert or uninhabited land'.[32] Stephen's complete about face was the result of working in the Colonial Office itself for ten years and watching the process of colonial expansion at close hand.

Questions relating to sovereignty confronted the settlers in the new colony of South Australia. The private members bill that established the colony was prefaced by the declaration that the large area of southern Australia was 'waste and unoccupied lands which are supposed fit for the purposes of colonisation'.[33] But it was widely understood, both in Britain and the new colony, that there was no unoccupied land. The critical legal question that quickly emerged was whether British law could be imposed on the Aboriginal nations living beyond the confines of the areas actually subject to settlement. South Australia's Governor George Gawler came to the conclusion that Aboriginal peoples in remote districts had to be considered as independent societies that should be judged by the law of nations. In an address to his executive council in September 1840, he sought to define the 'precise position in which the natives of this Province stand, in relation to the Government'. He explained that the current doctrine that 'they must be held and dealt with as British subjects, and, under no circumstances, to be tried or punished, except according to the ordinary forms of our law' could not 'be received without modification'. This was likely the case with those bands that lived close by the villages and the farms of the newcomers and had to a certain extent become incorporated into colonial society. He referred specifically to 'those tribes with whom we have constant and peaceful intercourse – for whose subsistence we provide – who acquiesce in, and acknowledge a friendly relation with us'.

But there was a quite different situation with distant tribes beyond the limits of our settlement

> with whom we have never communicated under friendly
> circumstances, whose language is equally unknown to us
> as ours is to them, and who betray, in all their intercourse
> with Europeans, the most savage and brutal hostility –
> who have never acknowledged subjection to any power,
> and who, indeed, seem incapable of being subjected to
> authority or deterred from atrocious crimes, except by
> military force. Nor can it be doubted that circumstances

may occur, in which, for the safety of the colonists, and for the prevention of plunder and bloodshed, it may be necessary to view such tribes ... however savage and barbarous their manners, as a *separate state or nation*, not acknowledging, but acting independently of, and in opposition to, British interests and authority.[34]

The South Australian chief justice, Sir Charles Cooper, adopted very similar views, distinguishing between the settled districts where the British had 'assumed a dominion ... in which the natives ... appeared to have acquiesced' and over those who lived beyond the frontiers, like the people of the Coorong, whom the Europeans knew as the Milmenrura tribe, and who were, he declared,

> a wild and savage tribe whose country, although within the limits of South Australia, has never been occupied by settlers – people who have never submitted themselves to our dominion, and between whom and the settlers there has been no social intercourse. It is a maxim of the English law, that no person is subject to be tried by it who does not owe some obedience to it ... I do not know how it can be said that the Milmenrura tribe owe any obedience whatever to the English law.[35]

The concurrence of the views of both the governor and chief justice is striking, and important for our understanding of the assertion of British sovereignty in colonial Australia. Both men accepted that Britain had claimed external sovereignty over Central Australia and that the coastline, both south and north, would be defended against a foreign rival. Internal sovereignty was a different matter. It only applied to what they termed settled areas – obviously Adelaide and small satellite villages, and the outer fringe of farms where the land was cultivated and fenced. These were districts where the European population had quickly outnumbered the local Indigenous bands. Everyone resident here was subject to the introduced legal code. As more immigrants arrived, the frontier of settlement was progressively thrust outward. But the implication was clear – sovereignty applied to those places where the Europeans were in actual occupation. Beyond there were an unknown number of 'separate states or nations'. And the area they occupied reached through the centre of the continent and 2500 kilometres away into the tropics. The British were in effective control of considerably less than 10 per cent of Central Australia, and probably made up an even smaller percentage of the population.

When the new colony was founded in 1836, British settlement in Australia was nearly fifty years old. Imperial policy towards Australia had undergone considerable change in that time. Colonial experience had rapidly undermined the views and the legal doctrine brought from London in 1788. The continent was not a land without people. Every exploring expedition that ventured inland during that half-century returned with reports of previously uncontacted nations. It became obvious, too, that Aboriginal bands lived in clearly defined areas and that they were in effective occupation of their ancestral homelands. All of this ethnographic information fortified the humanitarian movement ascendant in Britain after the reform of parliament in 1832 and the abolition of slavery in the following year. The violent conflict in Tasmania between 1827 and 1831 drew attention to the consequences of proceeding with colonisation without treaties to deal with the linked problems of sovereignty and property. Colonial officials called for the negotiation of treaties, and the imperial government made the significant decision to negotiate with the Māori at the very start of the settlement of New Zealand in 1840.

George Arthur, governor of Tasmania from 1824 to 1836, strongly impressed on the Colonial Office the need to negotiate treaties in future settlements in Australia. In a dispatch of 1832 he insisted that it was 'a fatal error in the first settlement of Van Diemen's Land that a treaty was not entered into with the natives, of which savages well comprehend the nature'.[36] He followed up three years later observing: 'On the first occupation of the colony it was a great oversight that a treaty was not, at that time, made with the natives, and such compensation given to the chiefs as they would have deemed a fair equivalent for what they surrendered ...'[37] Arthur's contemporaries advocated similar policies. In 1836, Colonel FC Irwin, commandant of the small military force in the Swan River Colony, now Perth, observed that all future dealings with the Aboriginal peoples should be governed by treaties negotiated between the two parties as a 'measure of healing and pacification'.[38]

The question of sovereignty was, then, an abiding concern in the early years of British colonisation. It has remained a matter of contention ever since. Australia is now challenged by the assertion in the Uluru Statement from the Heart that the Aboriginal and Islander peoples were the first sovereign nations of the continent, that 'it has never been ceded or extinguished and co-exists with the sovereignty of the Crown'. This is a particularly contentious proposition challenging fundamental legal doctrine. But as we have seen, the historical record indicates that the case presented in the Statement from the Heart is far stronger than many people imagine, and the traditional legal position far less imposing than it appears.

3

WHOSE LAND?

In a major case fought about Aboriginal land rights in the Northern Territory Supreme Court in 1971, Justice Maurice Blackburn declared that 'on the foundation of New South Wales ... and of South Australia, every square inch of territory in the colony became the property of the Crown'.[1] In an earlier High Court case, Justice Isaac Isaacs was more emphatic, pushing the date of expropriation even further back asserting that: 'we start with the unquestionable position that, when Governor Phillip received his first Commission from King George III. on 12th October 1786, the whole of the lands of Australia were already in law the *property* of the King of England'.[2]

It is hard to know where to begin. The expropriation of about 400 million hectares of land over half a continent was an act of theft on a truly heroic scale. It no doubt seemed more plausible and justifiable in London six months before the First Fleet left for the antipodes than at any later time. Experience in Australia rapidly undermined the moral and the legal case for the action of the Crown. Within fifty years the extravagance of the claim was fully exposed and widely understood. And yet the law was impervious to change. It remained frozen in that moment of expropriation, still guiding Australian judges 200 years after the arrival of the First Fleet. And it mattered every moment of those two centuries. It mattered everywhere over the vast landmass. The original act of expropriation was by any measure the most disastrous decision in Australia's history.

Conflict over land began with the British arrival. It was recapitulated wherever the colonists pushed their way into the territory of the First Nations onto land they believed they had both a moral and a legal right to occupy. The need of sheep and cattle for water and grass everywhere took precedence, and as a direct result the Indigenous land owners were driven away from their own carefully managed hunting ranges. The accompanying violence was ever present, though it varied greatly in intensity and duration depending on time and terrain. But frontier conflict, as it is now generally known, was an irresistible accompaniment of Australian colonisation from the late 18th to the early 20th century.

Too close a focus on the conflict itself distracts attention that should remain on the original act of expropriation. Policy was determined in Britain. The colonists had little say on such vital matters until the middle of the 19th century or until 1890 in Western Australia. And British law overshadowed the Australian courts and Australian life for much longer. Property law remained as it was in 1788 until the High Court's *Mabo* judgment in 1992. It was all part of the heavy burden of Empire about which Australians generally remained remarkably sanguine. Soft power it may have been, but it was anything but soft in its impact on the First Nations. And there was a cover of interwoven misconceptions that pointed critical thinking in quite the wrong direction. We have not escaped from them even now. Indeed, they can still be heard in contemporary discourse.

In their explanations of the pervasive power of *terra nullius*, legal historians have often swerved from criticism to complicity. In his standard work *International Law*, DP O'Connell argued in 1970 that Australia was treated as a land without owners 'since the Australian Aborigines were held incapable of intelligent transactions with respect to land'.[3] In 1978, Professor JR Andrews declared that the reason Aboriginal rights were disregarded was the 'scattered, disorganized and extremely backward and inhibited nature of Aboriginal society'.[4] In 1970, the distinguished Australian jurist Elizabeth Evatt observed that:

> Australia is in fact one of the rare examples of a large tract of inhabited territory acquired peaceably by occupation without any consent being sought from the native population. There is a practical explanation for this, for although a state might prefer to obtain some form of consent where there is an organized community with a recognized chief, this was impossible in Australia, inhabited by scattered unorganized tribes.[5]

In *The Creation of States in International Law*, eminent jurist James Crawford observed that *terra nullius* could only apply to territory occupied by 'nomadic groups lacking all regular political organization'. The number of places that could be so defined were, he explained, 'very few indeed'. Only Australia and the South Island of New Zealand were 'treated as falling within that category, apart from scattered islands or totally uninhabited tracts'.[6]

A troubling feature of these comments from the 1960s and 1970s is what appears to be the almost complete lack of familiarity with and perhaps disinterest in Australian history or anthropology. More disturbing is the underlying assumption that the British decision to treat Australia as a *terra nullius* was understandable and perhaps even appropriate. It was not, the argument runs, the result of a disastrous British mistake, but a consequence of the failure of Aboriginal society to attain a designated level of 'civilisation'. It seems inescapable that underlying these interpretations was the view surviving from an earlier era that the Indigenous Australians were a uniquely primitive people. This is scarcely surprising. Such views have been deeply embedded in Australian popular culture for a very long time. They disappeared from legal discourse as far back as the 1970s but they still have a half-life in the wider community.

A popular and comforting idea is that British policy was both morally acceptable and legally sound at the time. It is, the argument goes, just the way things were done in the 18th century, and it is anachronistic to judge the past by contemporary standards. It appears plausible. But it can only be sustained in the absence of any understanding of either international or the common law or, for that matter, the accepted practice among the imperial powers at the time that Cook sailed along the east coast of Australia and the first colony was planted on the shores of Sydney Harbour. The simplest explanation that is frequently adduced for the expropriation of the property of every Indigenous nation is that the British conquered Australia and thereby acquired both the sovereignty and the property in one apocalyptic moment. The First Nations lost their land because they were unable to defend it. It is an argument that seemingly has a simple strength, but it would have scandalised 18th-century jurists.

Emmerich de Vattel was the most widely read international lawyer of the time and was well known and often quoted in colonial Australia. In his 1758 *Law of Nations*, he explained that 'The conqueror takes possession of the property of the State and leaves that of individuals untouched.' The citizens caught up in a war of conquest suffer only indirectly because it 'merely brings them a change of sovereigns'.[7] Chief Justice John Marshall of the American Supreme Court outlined the law as it was understood at the time in a judgment delivered in 1833, explaining:

> It was very unusual, even in cases of conquest, for the conqueror to do more than displace the sovereign and assume dominion over the country. The modern usage of nations, which has become law, would be violated; that sense of justice and right which is acknowledged and felt by the whole civilized world would be outraged if private property should be generally confiscated, and private rights annulled. The people change their alliance; their relations to their ancient sovereign is dissolved, but their

relations to each other, and their rights of property remain undisturbed.[8]

A second common misconception is that the Aboriginal peoples were not in possession of the lands through which they travelled. They had not fully established their ownership. Without some form of agriculture, their land rights could not be recognised and they should make way for people who would use the land more productively. This has been a widely canvassed view in Australia, despite the vast accumulation of ethnographic information from as far back as the 1790s that has established beyond reasonable doubt that the Indigenous Australians were indeed land owners who used their country in a great diversity of ways, as Bruce Pascoe has explained in his recent bestselling book *Dark Emu*.[9] This was the conclusion made by Philip Gidley King, the third governor of New South Wales. When he was preparing to leave the colony in 1807, he drafted a memo for his successor, William Bligh, in which he observed, apropos the Aboriginal peoples, that he had 'ever considered them the real proprietors of the soil'.[10] Succeeding governors came to the same conclusion. In 1821, while discussing the Aboriginal inhabitants with a pioneer missionary, Governor Sir Thomas Brisbane remarked that 'we have taken the land from the Aborigines of the country and a remuneration ought to be made'.[11] Tasmania's Governor Arthur agreed, arguing that the utmost care should be taken in providing reparation 'for whatever land is taken possession of by the British settlers; for as each tribe claims some portion of territory, which they consider peculiarly their own, they should be in some formal manner satisfied for bartering it away; a negotiation which they perfectly comprehend'.[12]

The idea that only farmers who worked the land on which they lived could have title to their land still haunts popular culture. It had little purchase in the law of the 18th century or in practical land management. Britain was closely settled but there were large areas that had never known the plough, either because the land was unsuitable or because it was reserved for hunting or forestry or even the large ornamental parks of the aristocracy. The common law contained no provisions that encouraged land owners to make particular use of their land. Even sporadic use was sufficient to establish continuing occupancy. Shooting over land reserved for hunting a few times a year was also sufficient. High country used for seasonal grazing remained in the hand of its owners even if left empty for much of the year.

International law of the late 18th and early 19th centuries provided even stronger support to the rights of communities actually in possession of land, regardless of their manner of living. In his book *The Law of Nations*, first published in 1788, GF von Martens observed: 'If possession be immemorial, if there exists no possession anterior to it; it is undoubtedly sufficient to set aside all the pretensions of others ... founded upon the duration of this possession, it is the consequence of the natural impossibility of any other to prove a right better founded than that of possession.'[13]

The international law of possession was given its definitive interpretation by Frederick Carl von Savigny in his *Treatise on Possession* first published in 1803. There were four basic principles. To begin with, 'Possession, independent of all right, is the foundation of property.' In any conflict over property, the possessor had the benefit of the burden of proof being thrown on his adversary. Presence on the land in question was the fundamental first step in acquiring possession, and beyond that it was 'only necessary to be *present on the land*, without the performance of any other act thereon'. But there must also be the will to maintain ownership, the *animus possidendi*. Consequently possession could only be lost when land was physically abandoned. This did not apply to land which was only used at certain times like alpine pastures, von Savigny explaining: 'Where the user is of such a nature, that it only recurs at certain periods: whoever during the interval omits to visit the [land], does not thereby manifest any intention of giving up the Possession.'[14]

International law as it was understood in the 18th century was much more sympathetic to tribal societies that lived by hunting and herding than was commonly the case a hundred years later. A case in point is Christian Wolff's *The Law of Nations*, first published in 1750. Included in this massive work of scholarship was a consideration of the rights of peoples such as the Aboriginal Australians who lived in small groups moving regularly across land owned collectively under what he termed 'mixed community holding'. If the families had,

> no settled abode but wander through the uncultivated
> wilds ... they are understood to have tacitly agreed that
> the lands in that territory in which they change their
> abodes as they please are held in common, subject to the

use of individuals, and it is not to be doubted but that it is
their intention that they should not be deprived of that use
by outsiders. Therefore they are supposed to have occupied
that territory as far as concerns the lands subject to their
use, and consequently to have jointly acquired ownership
of those lands, so that the use of them belongs to all
without distinction.[15]

The views of a German scholar were one thing; policy
of the British government was quite another. Six years after
Wolff's work was published, a royal proclamation was issued
dealing with the political and geographical fallout from the
Seven Years War in North America. It determined new
boundaries and included important provisions regarding the
Native American nations. All the country beyond the water-
sheds of the Appalachian Mountains was reserved for the
Native Americans. Elsewhere, Native American property
rights were recognised and could only be ceded or sold to the
Crown or, as the document declared:

It is just and reasonable, and essential to Our Interest and
the Security of Our Colonies, that the several Nations
or Tribes of Indians, with whom We are connected, and
who live under Our Protection, should not be molested
or disturbed in the Possession of such Parts of Our
Dominions and Territories as, not having been ceded to,
or purchased by Us, are reserved to them, as their Hunting
Grounds ...[16]

The proclamation has been seen, ever since, as establishing legal precedents that are still relevant to common law jurisdictions. In one of Canada's most important native title cases, *Calder v Attorney-General of British Columbia* of 1973, Justice Emmett Hall explained that: 'Its force as a statute is analogous to the status of Magna Carta which has always been considered to be the law throughout the Empire. It was a law which followed the flag as England assumed jurisdiction over newly discovered or acquired lands or territories.'[17]

There was marked continuity between the Native American policy of the British Empire and of the new American republic, which can be seen in the 1787 Northwest Ordinance dealing with the government of territory beyond the boundaries of the founding states of the union. Article three referred to the resident Native Americans. It can be usefully compared with Phillip's instructions issued in London three months earlier. Both documents expressed good will. Phillip was urged to 'conciliate their affections, enjoining all our subjects to live in amity and kindness with them'.[18] Colonising Americans were instructed to always act with 'utmost good faith' in order to preserve 'peace and friendship with them'. Congress determined that the Native Americans had a form of title, and that land and property would 'never be taken from them without their consent'.[19] Phillip's instructions had nothing whatever to say about Aboriginal property rights.

The American Supreme Court, led by Chief Justice John Marshall from 1801 to 1835, developed the most authoritative definition of Indian or Native title in a series of famous judgments. They were all of great relevance to Australian jurisprudence. In *Worcester v Georgia*, Marshall began with the proposition that before the arrival of the Europeans, America had been 'inhabited by a distinct people', who had institutions of their own and governed themselves by their own laws. 'It is difficult', he declared, 'to comprehend the proposition that the inhabitants of either quarter of the globe could have rightful original claims of dominion over the inhabitants of the other, or over the lands they occupied; or that discovery of either by the other should give the discoverer rights in the country discovered which annulled the pre-existing rights of its ancient possessors.'[20] As if to answer the claims made by the British over eastern Australia in 1788, Marshall observed that it was an 'extravagant and absurd idea that the feeble settlements made on the seacoast ... acquired legitimate power ... to govern the people, or occupy the lands from sea to sea'. All that the settlers acquired was 'the exclusive right of purchasing such lands as the natives were willing to sell'.

In *Johnson v McIntosh* in 1823, Marshall declared that the Native Americans were 'admitted to be the rightful occupants of the soil, with a legal as well as just claim to retain possession of it'. It had 'never been contended that the Indian title amounted to nothing'. Indeed, their right of possession had 'never been questioned'.[21] The American courts did not distinguish between different forms of land use or declare that hunting and gathering were not, somehow, legitimate forms of land management. In 1826, Marshall remarked that:

Indian possession or occupation was considered with
reference to their habits and modes of life; their hunting

grounds were as much in their actual possession as the cleared fields of the whites; and their rights to its exclusive enjoyment in their own way and for their own purposes were as much respected until they … made a cession to the government, or an authorized sale to individuals.[22]

Native title as defined in the Marshall Supreme Court was taken up in New Zealand courts in the leading case *The Crown v Symonds* in 1847. Justice HS Chapman remarked that it secured to the Māori 'all the enjoyments from the land' that they had before the arrival of the Europeans. Whatever the opinion of jurists as to the strength or weakness of native title, it was 'entitled to be respected' and it could not be extinguished 'otherwise than by the free consent of the native occupiers'. Chapman explained that the concept had a long history:

The intercourse of civilized nations, and especially of Great Britain, with the aboriginal natives of America and other countries, during the last two centuries, has gradually led to the adoption and affirmation by the Colonial Courts, of certain established principles of law, applicable to such intercourse. Although these principles may at times have been lost sight of … our Colonial Courts, and the Courts of such of the United States of America as have adopted the common law of England, have invariably affirmed and supported them; so that at this day, a line of judicial decision, the current of legal opinion, and above all, the settled practice of Colonial Governments, have concurred to clothe with certainty and precision what would otherwise have remained vague and unsettled.[23]

Chapman had spent time in Canada and had developed an understanding of native title from that experience. It is not clear if he appreciated the extent to which the Australian colonies had not so much 'lost sight' of native title but had never seen it in the first place. When he moved to Tasmania in 1852, however, he would have learnt about the tragic fate of the island's Aboriginal peoples and may even have read John West's powerful account of the violent conflict in his two volume *History of Tasmania* published that year in Launceston.

The Tasmanian story played an important part in the rapid evolution of British policy in the 1830s, particularly with the coming to power of Lord Melbourne's Whig administration in May 1835, which greatly increased the influence of the powerful humanitarian lobby in the Colonial Office. It was an auspicious moment for reformers of colonial policy, because after bringing about the abolition of slavery all over the Empire in 1833, leading activists like Thomas Buxton turned their attention to the fate of the Indigenous peoples in British colonies. Buxton had learnt a great deal about the brutal conflict in Tasmania, both from official papers printed by the House of Commons and from correspondents on the island. 'I protest', he wrote, 'I hate shooting innocent savages worse than slavery itself.'[24] George Arthur, who returned to Britain in 1836, continued to argue that violence was inevitable unless there was an acceptance of Indigenous property rights, and this view was widely shared among British humanitarians.

The high point of humanitarian interest in tribal people came with the work of the House of Commons Select Committee on Aborigines (British Settlements) chaired by Buxton, which issued reports in 1836 and 1837. Australia received considerable attention, members noting that within the 'recollection of many living men every part of this territory was the undisputed property of the Aborigines'. But in the establishment of the colonies it did not appear that 'the territorial rights of the natives were considered'. In fact, Aboriginal claims 'whether as sovereigns or proprietors of the soil, have been utterly disregarded'. 'The land had been taken from them without the assertion of any other title than that of superior force.' In his report, Buxton observed that:

> It might be presumed that the native inhabitants of any land have an incontrovertible right to their own soil: a plain and sacred right, however, which seems not to have been understood. Europeans have entered their borders uninvited, and, when there, have not only acted as if they were undoubted lords of the soil, but have punished the natives as aggressors if they have evinced a disposition to live in their own country.

More than anything else, this was a direct condemnation of the policies that had been implemented in the Australian colonies since 1788.[25]

The change of both personnel and policy in the Colonial Office came at a bad time for the promoters of the new colony in South Australia, who had been working on the assumption that they would be able to follow the precedent of New South Wales and Tasmania, and disregard the property rights of the resident Aboriginal peoples. It was a fair assumption to make. But Secretary of State Lord Glenelg, his deputy Sir George Grey and departmental head James Stephen had other ideas. The government's commitment to native title found expression in letters patent prepared for the new colony, which included a clause reading: 'Providing always, that nothing in these our Letters Patent contained shall affect or be constrained to affect the rights of any Aboriginal natives of the said Province to the actual occupation or employment in their persons or in the persons of their descendants of any lands now actually occupied or enjoyed by such Natives.'[26] Lord Glenelg called Robert Torrens, the chairman of the South Australian Commission, into the Colonial Office and informed him of the conditions that were to be imposed on the settlers before final approval was to be given for the ships to depart for the antipodes. The commissioners were to 'prepare a plan for securing the rights of the Aborigines which plan should include the appointment of a Colonial Officer to be called Protector of the Aborigines and arrangements for purchasing the lands of the Natives'.[27]

It was a moment of historical importance. Fifty years after the arrival of the First Fleet the imperial government had officially cast aside the idea of *terra nullius*. The Aboriginal peoples were the proprietors of their traditional lands. Settlement had to involve the purchase of such lands as they were willing to surrender. It was a sudden and dramatic about turn. Only a few years before, the Act of parliament establishing the colony had declared that the land in question was waste and unoccupied. Robert Torrens was aware that history was on his side, observing that hitherto in the colonisation of Australia the 'case of native occupancy' had 'never yet been provided for'.[28] The commissioners of the colony realised that they had to give every appearance of agreeing with the reformers in the Colonial Office in order to proceed with the project, while all the while realising that South Australia was a long way from Downing Street. And there was always the question of who would determine what Aboriginal property rights amounted to. Torrens chose his words with great care, promising on numerous occasions to protect 'the Natives in the unmolested exercise of their rights of property in Land'. But then came the critical qualification: 'should such a right be anywhere found to exist'.[29] And he did not believe it did. He later explained that he thought the Aboriginal peoples were 'unlocated', and indeed that property in land was 'utterly unknown to them' because the wandering tribes 'never held a single acre in permanent occupation'.[30]

The First Nations of South Australia and the Northern Territory did not significantly benefit as a result of the well-meaning endeavours of Britain's humanitarian reformers. Small reserves of land were set aside for them but they were of little practical use. Parties of overlanders from New South Wales brought sheep and cattle to the new colony, along with their guns and the entrenched brutality of the frontier wars that had been raging around the ravelled frontiers of settlement for forty years. A South Australian clergyman wrote home to England in 1840 of a co-religionist who since arriving in the colony had 'adopted the opinions of the other Overland

Desperadoes who glorify in shooting the blacks'.[31] When local colonists pushed out into the interior, their behaviour had become assimilated with that of the 'other siders', who knew how to handle the troublesome tribesmen.

The arrival in South Australia of these parties from New South Wales was just one manifestation of the extraordinary mobility of colonial society. Restraints put in place by the government of New South Wales were swept aside, and in a little more than a decade squatters and their sheep and cattle spilt out into the vast hinterland, occupying land along all the river frontages. They advanced southward to the Murray and into Port Phillip, where they met the Tasmanians who had brought their sheep penned on the decks of small ketches sailing out of Launceston. The thrust to the north was even more dramatic, with parties pushing up over the Liverpool Plains and intruding onto the Darling Downs in the early 1840s. The squatting rush as it became known was a unique challenge to the Colonial Office. Such a rapid expansion was neither welcome nor expected. There was no precedent for it. The best that could be done to assert some authority was to impose a system of pastoral licences to prevent the squatters from eventually claiming freehold rights as a result of long occupation.

The challenge to the Aboriginal peoples was even more severe, sparking savage conflict all along a frontier stretching thousands of kilometres. Intense pressure from the squatters and their urban friends and financiers to be given greater security of tenure resulted in a system of pastoral leases. How these impacted on the besieged First Nations was played out in Port Phillip, where the recently appointed Aboriginal protectors watched on with impotent alarm. When Chief Protector GA Robinson arrived in Melbourne, he visited the office of the surveyor-general, who showed him a map where the land was parcelled out in huge allotments and 'not a single reserve for the blacks'. He wrote in his private journal: 'There is a complete system of expulsion and Extermination for the first Purchaser of their lands drive them on the other Purchased lands and then on ad infinitum.'[32]

The local courts were no help, having determined that a pastoralist holding a licence from the government could drive 'trespassing' Aboriginal groups off the land in question by any means in their power. Robinson returned to the subject in his annual reports sent to Sydney and eventually passed on to the Colonial Office. In his report of 1846 he explained that with all the discussion about security of tenure for the pastoralists there was never any mention of the claim of the Aboriginal peoples 'to a reasonable share in the Soil of their fatherland'. He incorporated a letter he had received from the assistant protector, ES Parker, who declared that very soon every acre of traditional land would be so leased out and occupied as to leave them, 'in a legal view, no place for their feet'. He feared that the 'unfortunate natives might be hunted from Station to Station, without a Spot they can call their own'.[33]

Robinson's anxious appeal evoked no response when it was read in Sydney, if indeed it was read at all. But when it reached the Colonial Office it was a different story. The first official who read it minuted that it would be 'most unjust that the Natives should be extruded in the manner described ... from the soil of which till recently they were the sole occupants'. And the concern grew as Robinson's report passed up the office hierarchy, eventually arriving on the desk of the secretary of state Earl Grey, who wrote that Governor Charles Fitzroy must be instructed that the Aboriginal inhabitants were not to be driven off the pastoral stations and that sufficient land should be reserved 'with a view to their preservation from being exterminated'.[34]

Grey struggled with the problem of how to provide Aboriginal access to land given the distinctive nature of both Aboriginal and the squatter's use of what in European eyes were vast areas. The traditional creation of many small reserves was not appropriate; he explained in a dispatch to Governor Fitzroy that

> the very difficulty of thus locating the Aboriginal
> Tribes absolutely apart from the Settlers renders it
> more incumbent on Government to prevent them from
> being altogether excluded from the land under pastoral
> occupation. I think it essential that it should be generally
> understood that leases granted for this purpose give the
> grantees only an exclusive right of pasturage for their
> cattle, and of cultivating such land as they may require
> within the large limits thus assigned to them, but that
> leases are not intended to deprive the natives of their
> former right to hunt over these Districts, or to wander over
> them in search of subsistence, in the manner to which they
> have been heretofore accustomed, from the spontaneous
> produce of the soil ...[35]

In 1849 the means were found to insert in pastoral leases in New South Wales clauses that provided the required protection, and similar provisions were included in the leases granted in South Australia and Western Australia. In February 1850, Grey doubled down on his defence of Aboriginal rights and in a dispatch to Governor Fitzroy reminded him that 'the practice of driving the Natives from the cattle runs is illegal, and they have every right to the protection of the law from such aggressions'. And it was not to be taken lightly. Indeed it was a matter 'of very great importance'.[36]

A few months after writing this dispatch, Grey informed his Australian governors that the Colonial Office was preparing legislation that would grant internal self-government to New South Wales, South Australia, Tasmania and the new colony of Victoria. After sixty years, responsibility for the First Nations was to be passed over to the colonists themselves sitting in their new bicameral parliaments. With a sense of foreboding, Grey reminded them that in 'assuming their territories the Settlers [had] incurred a moral obligation of the most sacred kind'. The honour of both imperial and colonial governments was 'deeply concerned in proving that no effort [had] been wanting on their part to avert the destruction of the Native Races as a consequence of occupation of their territories by British subjects'.[37]

But even in 1856 when the new colonial parliaments opened their doors, at least half the continent was still in the possession of the First Nations. This was obviously the case in the tropical north, which came under the control of Queensland, South Australia and Western Australia, the last of which continued to be administered by the Colonial Office until 1890. The colonists' grasp of the country was by no means complete, and much of it was the result of the pastoral industry, which occupied vast provinces with a remarkably small number of Europeans. With a continent of such a size there were bound to be questions about the effectiveness of British control when considered in the light of international law.

4

EFFECTIVE CONTROL?

During the seventy years between 1786 and 1856, the fate of Australia's First Nations was determined by British officials, very few of whom had ever been in the country. But they were usually kept well informed by their colonial governors, whose regular dispatches frequently included attachments dealing with the minutiae of local administration. The Colonial Office bureaucrats who had oversight of Australian affairs developed a wide knowledge of what was going on in each of the colonies, so that by the end of the period they often had a broader understanding of continental developments than the settlers themselves, whose outlooks and experience were confined to their own colonies.

Colonial Office knowledge and interest in the Aboriginal peoples fluctuated, but it was an ever present subject in the immense volume of correspondence that crossed the world's oceans – copperplate writing on reams of pale blue paper neatly bundled and tied with thin pink tape. The men who read and wrote the dispatches worked in close proximity with colleagues who were dealing with developments in many other parts of the world and the impact of the Empire on what they termed 'native people' in Africa, the Americas and the Pacific.

The decision to establish a penal settlement on the east coast of New Holland was made in a hurry with remarkably little local knowledge, unlike many other parts of the world, where Europeans had visited and lived for 200 or 300 years. Information provided by members of the *Endeavour* voyage hindered rather than helped the development of appropriate policy towards the Aboriginal peoples, overriding experience gained in North America since the first half of the 17th century. As we have seen, two fateful decisions were made and embodied in the official instructions given to Phillip in 1786 and formally proclaimed by him at Sydney Cove on 7 February 1788. First, the British claimed sovereignty over the eastern half of the continent on the assumption that there was no pre-existing sovereignty either because the land was empty or because the local tribes were too scattered and disorganised to have exercised any recognisable form of governance. The second decision was to declare that from the date that Phillip was handed his instructions, or perhaps more likely from their formal proclamation in Australia, all the land became the property of the Crown because there were no prior proprietors. So with the truly big decisions already made, there was no need to seek a treaty with the First Nations. They had nothing to bring to the negotiating table, nothing to trade with. And while conflict might result, it could not be about land or territory, the universal objectives of warfare. The big strategic decisions had already been made.

Much had changed by the early 1850s as the British government prepared to transfer power to the colonial parliaments. Local knowledge had rapidly undermined the assumptions made before the expedition's departure. There were far more Aboriginal inhabitants, they lived in well-defined home-lands, and they remained there when the British intruded and resisted the invasion whenever they could. The more percep-tive settlers soon realised that the hinterland was not empty and that the locals gave every indication that they had a form of proprietorship and of sovereignty. So from that time on, the legal foundations of the colony were unsound and remain so to this day.

Aboriginal resistance was confronting from the start. Were the Aboriginal people subjects, and therefore 'in the King's peace', who should be treated according to the normal procedures of the criminal law when they attacked people or property? Or was it necessary to use terror to repress their vio-lence? It was a dilemma that confronted all the early gover-nors in New South Wales, Tasmania and Western Australia. The imperial government eventually responded in 1825 with the instructions to treat insurgent bands as though they were representatives of a foreign enemy. But this policy was quietly discarded in the 1830s. When Governor Arthur's dispatches were published in House of Commons Papers, his reference to and quotation of the 1825 instructions were removed. In 1837 the Colonial Office under Lord Glenelg turned policy back to where it had been in 1788. In a dispatch to New South Wales governor Richard Bourke, he declared that

> all the natives inhabiting those Territories must be
> considered as Subjects of the Queen, and as within H.M.'s
> Allegiance. To regard them as Aliens with whom a War

can exist, and against whom H.M.'s Troops may exercise belligerent right, is to deny that protection to which they derive the highest possible claim from the Sovereignty which has been assumed over the whole of their Ancient Possessions.[1]

Governor Gipps reaffirmed this doctrine in a proclamation issued in Sydney in May 1839 explaining that the Aboriginal peoples were indeed subjects of the Queen and had an 'equal right with people of European origin to the protection and assistance of the Law of England'. In every case where they suffered a violent death in fighting with the settlers there should be an inquest or inquiry.[2]

They were fine words, but they paid little regard to the realities of colonial society or its history since 1788. Many Indigenous Australians had been killed in fighting along the moving frontiers of settlement. There had been very few inquests or inquiries and even fewer prosecutions. The governors themselves had dispatched punitive expeditions to strike terror among insurgent bands. And the 'further out' the frontiersmen moved the weaker the grasp of government. At the time of Glenelg's edict, the squatting rush was at its height and the whole of south-eastern Australia was being overrun with vast flocks of sheep and herds of cattle driven forward by their well-armed owners and keepers. So the assertion that 'protection' was the most significant manifestation of British sovereignty undermines the whole argument about the reach of the Crown's authority. As we have already seen, the idea that British sovereignty enveloped the whole continent was not taken seriously in the Colonial Office itself. And in South Australia, both governors and judges believed that the introduced legal code only reached as far as closer settlement, and that the Aboriginal nations out in the vast hinterland had to be thought of as independent nations to be managed by international, not domestic law.

Perhaps even more pertinent was the fact that there had always been colonists who thought they were at war with the Aboriginal peoples. And this included everyone from governors and military officers down. References to war intruded into official correspondence, newspaper editorials and letters from correspondents, speeches at public meetings, and no doubt in innumerable private conversations. There was therefore a profound misalignment between law and life. Where it really mattered was when the settlers had to decide whether it was legitimate to kill Aboriginal people. If the various administrations had declared war, the moral burden would have been assumed by governors, their high officials and military officers. But the Crown law authorities in Britain had shut off that ethical slip-road.

The Indigenous Australians were subjects of the Crown, and killing them was murder even if rarely punished. And there was the rub! Because the colonial governments rarely attempted to bring colonists to justice, the community consensus was that killing 'blacks' was justified in almost any circumstances and that there was no moral equivalent between shooting them and murdering a countryman. The idea of justified homicide quickly took root in colonial society and became an intrinsic part of an evolving Australian folklore.

To many it seemed to be what was, in effect, a local law, which applied on the frontiers of settlement no matter what the officials or religious leaders had to say. There was, from the earliest times, community solidarity to keep any knowledge of killing hidden from outsiders, to protect perpetrators and revile and even rough up informers. Many officials lamented the conspiracy of silence they confronted and the related impossibility of persuading juries to convict even in the face of compelling evidence.

But it was a religious age and violent frontier conflict troubled many Christians. In some pulpits, clergymen promised divine retribution for shedding blood. It would, they declared, fall on individuals and the nation alike. Many lay Christians took up the Indigenous cause and wrote anguished letters to the newspapers and the powerful missionary societies in Britain. But making people feel guilty and even sinful was not a way to achieve popularity. The venom of attacks on the humanitarian lobby was a clear indication of how disturbing their advocacy often was. The colonists reserved their deepest scorn for the British humanitarian movement, for Exeter Hall as it was called, after the central meeting place of the Anti-Slavery Society in London. It was not just the censorious judgments that stung, but the fact that they emanated from Britain. It was interference from overseas from people who knew nothing about the inescapable realities of colonial life. By this time Australia and Britain were already on divergent paths. The anti-slavery crusade had mobilised a mass movement, and the enthusiasm, elan and organisation had provided humanitarian causes with a momentum that passed Australia by.

The most contentious debate swirled around the Christian doctrine of racial equality, the inescapable message of the Bible that all people were 'of one blood' and all alike capable of salvation. It was a troubling idea for a society that was dispossessing and killing the traditional owners. Racial ideas took root and grew strongly. Old stories about savages merged with new theories of racial hierarchies to produce a potent brew that eased the colonial conscience. If it could be established that the Aboriginal peoples were not fully human, then all the inbuilt restraints about homicide could be cast aside. Visitors from Britain and recent arrivals were shocked to discover the insouciance that had developed about shooting Aboriginal people. And that it was talked about even in the higher levels of colonial society, in the towns as well as out in the bush.

James Stephen in the Colonial Office read the dispatches from Australia with mounting alarm. In 1839, with constant news about conflict on the ever expanding pastoral frontier, he wrote a minute on a dispatch from Governor Gipps:

> The tendency of these collisions with the Blacks is
> unhappily too clear for doubt. They will ere long cease
> to be numbered amongst the Races of the Earth. I can
> imagine no law effective enough to avoid this result ...
> All this is most deplorable but I fear it is also inevitable.
> The only chance of saving them from annihilation would
> consist in teaching them the art of war and supplying them
> with weapons and munitions – an act of suicidal generosity
> which of course cannot be practised.[3]

Stephen also thought about the attitudes abounding in colonial society, referring to the 'hatred with which the white man regards the Black which resulted from fear – from the strong physical contrasts which intercept the sympathy which subsists between men of the same Race – from the consciousness of having done them great wrongs and from a desire to escape this painful reproach by laying the blame on the injured party'.[4]

Stephen's psychological insight was compelling, but his horror of developments in the colonies was underpinned by half-hidden hypocrisy. The disastrous turn of events in Australia needs to be placed in its true context. It arose as a direct consequence of the way the British arrived in Australia, overriding all existing property rights and ignoring the sovereignty of the First Nations. The Aboriginal peoples were treated with a total lack of respect. They were 'too primitive' to negotiate with and their ties to their homelands could be totally ignored. If the government treated them as scarcely human why would the ordinary people see things any differently? Fighting was the only way disputes about land could be resolved. Violence was implicit in British policy from the start. The gift of becoming a subject of the monarch meant nothing. Colonial governments had neither the will nor, more significantly, the capacity to shield the Aboriginal peoples from vigilante violence.

Concern in the Colonial Office was real enough. But it did not stand in the way of granting the colonies internal self-government and consequently abandoning the First Nations of eastern Australia to their fate. Stephen had left the Colonial Office in 1847 but he was a strong supporter of Canadian self-government and was a respected adviser as plans were made for the establishment of the Australian parliaments between 1856 and 1859. The one British legacy that was carried forward into the second half of the 19th century was the usufructuary or use rights inserted in pastoral leases all over Australia. The British Parliament legislated in 1855 to transfer to the colonists power over Crown land, but in doing so protected all interests already granted and placed them beyond the reach of the colonial parliaments. Ignored to a great extent for 150 years, the rights embodied in the pastoral leases were brought back to life by the High Court in the *Wik* case in 1996, to the surprise of the legal profession and the horror of the pastoral industry.

If the imperial government appeared to be surrendering the duty of care of the Aboriginal peoples, which they so often professed when they transferred power to the colonial capitals, their separation of Queensland from New South Wales in 1859 was positively reckless. The facts speak for themselves. There were less than 30 000 people in the colony. Settlement was concentrated in and around Brisbane, which was in the south-east corner. Pastoralists had already occupied the Darling Downs to the west of the new capital and land for a hundred kilometres or so to the north. But the fledgling government assumed responsibility over a vast landmass. Cape York was more than 2000 kilometres away; the western border, more than 1000 kilometres. The new government had little experience and less money. Knowledge of the vast hinterland was limited. Narrow ribbons of land seen and described by exploring expeditions in the 1840s did not amount to much.

It was obvious that there was a large Indigenous population, particularly along the coastline and in the broad river valleys. It was almost certain that there were many more Aboriginal people within Queensland's boundaries than colonists. It is likely that before the arrival of the British there were as many as 200,000 members of the First Nations, although by 1859 violence and disease had begun to scythe through the bands who had already confronted the invaders.

The new colony was almost totally dependent on the pastoral industry. It provided over 90 per cent of exports and many of the thin streams of revenue. The pastoralists and their urban allies controlled the new bicameral parliament. Two objectives dominated their deliberations. They sought to defend the vast estates they had already acquired, and they wanted to facilitate the rapid expansion of settlement. One of the new parliament's first pieces of legislation was the 1860 Land Bill, which allowed anyone to apply for a one-year lease to occupy a run of 100 square miles (260 square kilometres) and at the end of the year to apply for a fourteen-year lease dependent on reasonable efforts to stock the land in question. It drew in new settlers from the southern colonies now flush with gold-rush capital. Governor George Bowen celebrated the surge of settlement. He declared it 'almost sublime' to watch the 'margins of Christianity and Civilization' advance at a rate of 'some 200 miles' each year.[5] He watched with wonder 'the steady, silent flow of pastoral occupation over north-eastern Australia'. It resembled the 'rise of a tide or some other operation of nature, rather than a work of man'.[6]

It was, indeed, an astonishing expansion of settlement.

Within ten years the squatters had reached the base of Cape York, at which they swung west across the tropical savannah south of the Gulf of Carpentaria and by the 1880s had driven their cattle through the Northern Territory and into the East Kimberley, to eventually meet the Western Australian sheep farmers who had come north from the Gascoyne and Pilbara at much the same time. The circle of conquest had thus been completed. It had never been easy. Distance, drought, fire and flood had to be overcome. The further the pioneers went, the more distant the markets for their wool and beef, and prices fluctuated unpredictably. Generations of Australians were taught to admire their endurance and understated stoicism. They were winners in the heroic struggle against the land itself. This became the central narrative of the nation. The distinguished historian Keith Hancock remarked in his famous 1930 history of Australia that 'For six generations they [the settlers] have swarmed inland from the sea, pressing forward to their economic frontiers, which are the only frontiers Australia knows.'[7]

If only it was that easy. Like several generations of Australian historians, Hancock left the Aboriginal peoples out of the story. The high cost of the pastoral occupation of northern Australia was rarely mentioned. The heroic pioneers had blood on their hands and notches on the stocks of their rifles. It was in so many ways a terrible story. We still live with its consequences. And it leaves out the central question of Indigenous sovereignty. The hardy pioneers took Aboriginal lives, but did they actually conquer the north? To answer that question it will be instructive to consider the situation in 1901, when the new federal government was inaugurated and the first parliament met in Melbourne thousands of kilometres away on the far south-east coast.

One of the continuing concerns of the new federal politicians was the empty north. And they had a point. The squatters had flooded the tropical savannah with their sheep and cattle, but very few white men accompanied them and subsequently managed them. Outback stations become almost totally dependent on the labour of young Indigenous men and women. Perhaps as many as 10 000 worked for the white men in 1901. Typically, only a handful of European men and very few women lived in or near the stations' big houses. The Queensland tropical coast was the only place where there were substantial towns and intensive agriculture, and there were mining towns like Charters Towers in the hinterland. The big tropical towns – Cairns, Broome, Darwin – and Thursday Island had small European communities but they were usually outnumbered by mixed populations of Chinese, Japanese, Filipinos, Pacific Islanders and Indigenous Australians. And many of the white Australians were footloose, working for a while in the north before moving on, usually back to the south. There were habitual laments about the lack of white women but the prevailing view was that they could not flourish, let alone raise healthy children in the tropics. But perhaps even more significant was that in 1901 there were still many parts of the north where white men had rarely if ever been. The local people may have heard stories about the white men, but many would never have seen one. The sheep and cattle had overrun the open grasslands, but that was as far as they went, their progress stalled by rugged country, wetlands and desert. So traditional life went on largely undisturbed in much of Cape York, Arnhem Land, the Kimberley, the arid lands and the numerous offshore islands.

Edmund Barton, the first prime minister, famously declared that federation would create 'a nation for a continent and a continent for a nation'.[8] But a more compelling problem was whether the new parliament in Melbourne exercised effective control over vast areas of the continent in the way that was understood in international law and practice at the time. A more pressing and attendant question was whether the First Nations continued to exercise internal sovereignty based on their ancient laws and customs. In the debate on the Immigration Restriction Bill in 1901, Barton's colleague Alfred Deakin observed that the parliament was legislating for the future of the whole continent before the white Australians had 'effectively occupied a quarter' of it and 'with the great bulk of its immense extent little more than explored, or with a sparse settlement'. It would be for future generations 'to enter into and possess the country of which we at present only hold the border'.[9]

This was a telling comment. The question of effective control was of great importance in the late 19th and early 20th centuries as the great powers competed for trade and territory all over the world. It was a major question discussed at the Berlin International Conference of 1885, which met with the aim of providing principles that would allow for mediation between competing powers. The consensus arrived at was summarised by MF Lindley in the most relevant

20th-century text. Effective control over territory depended on 'The existence there of sufficient authority to protect life and property; and, so far as an absolute title is concerned, the broad rule is that the possessions of a Power extends as far as, and no further than, its administrative machinery is in efficient exercise.'[10] This would have been an impossible standard for Australia to reach in the early 20th century.

But it is important to appreciate that the British government applied these standards elsewhere in the world. In 1887, Lord Salisbury observed that it was by then admitted by all the major powers that a claim of sovereignty in Africa could only be sustained by a 'real occupation of the territory claimed'.[11] This was the reason used by Britain to refuse a Portuguese claim to territory in central Africa between its two colonies Angola and Mozambique, because 'in the greater part of the region there was no sign of Portuguese jurisdiction or authority; and he refused to recognize any claim to sovereignty which was not based on real occupation'.[12]

Britain had a similar dispute at much the same time with Nicaragua about the status of the Mosquito Indians (i.e. Miskito people) of the Atlantic coast and the sovereignty over the territory in question, which was taken to international mediation. Nicaragua argued that she was a successor state to the Spanish Empire and that her acquired sovereignty was, therefore, unquestioned and had been settled for many years. As for the Miskito, they clearly lived within the internationally acknowledged boundaries of the republic and were too 'primitive' to exercise any degree of independence. They lived by hunting and fishing and, Nicaragua claimed, were without arts, law or religion or any of the other attributes of a regular society. Britain argued that Nicaragua could not claim 'an absolute sovereignty' but one only of a 'qualified and limited order'.[13] This was a consequence of the fact that neither Spain nor Nicaragua had 'actually exercised the pretended rightful sovereignty'. They had never taken possession 'in fact'. The Miskito were therefore able to maintain their actual freedom and to operate as a separate community because their incorporation into the Nicaraguan Republic was 'a relative and incomplete incorporation'. The mediation ended up supporting the British position.[14]

This case had direct relevance to Australia. Given the vast size of the continent, many First Nations were in exactly the same situation as the Miskito people, although the latter had been the nominal subjects of Spanish/Nicaraguan sovereignty for much longer than the Aboriginal incorporation into the British Empire. The authority of the colonial governments was 'clearly of a qualified and limited order'. They had never taken possession of large swathes of territory 'in fact'. The clear implication of international law and practice was that the Aboriginal peoples in northern Australia had been subject at best to 'a relative and incomplete incorporation'. And then there was the inability of the Australian governments to protect the Aboriginal people from widespread violence, from what was legally large-scale murder.

Lindley explained that in the 'early stages' of colonial rule it was often thought that to maintain order it was necessary to conduct punitive military expeditions. But the requirements of effective occupation clearly involved 'on the part of the acquiring State ... taking steps to secure the administration and policing of the whole territory under its full sovereignty or protection so as to render it possible, within a reasonable time, to mete out punishment to the guilty individually'.[15] In the north until well into the 20th century, however, governments continued to conduct or allow punitive expeditions and were unable or unwilling to take action to protect Aboriginal communities from the depredations of the frontiersmen.

The government resident for the Northern Territory addressed the problem in a report to the South Australian parliament in 1898, in which he confessed that it was impossible to stop white men kidnapping and raping Aboriginal women:

> Considering the vast area of country, sparsely populated, over which it is utterly impossible to maintain control, it is difficult indeed to suggest any remedy which would *effectually* cope with the evil which undoubtedly exists. Those who occupy the 'back blocks' are, in most cases, a law unto themselves as regards their relations with the natives.[16]

And at the same time many Aboriginal communities were far out of the reach of the authorities. After a tour of the Northern Territory in 1905, the governor of South Australia, Sir GR Le Hunte, observed that only a small fraction of the Aboriginal population was 'under any control' or indeed 'in any contact with any form of Government or civilization'.[17] The situation had not greatly changed on the eve of the Second World War. In 1940 the protector of Aborigines, JA Carrodus, wrote to the administrator of the Northern

Territory, referring to the 'relatively uncivilized natives' who lived 'more or less permanently in remote areas, who are not under any form of permanent European control, assistance or supervision, and who depend for internal stability on the free exercise of their own native customs'.[18]

If we apply the standards of international law as they were understood at the time of Australian federation, neither the states nor the federal government exercised effective control over large areas of the continent. The conquest of the north was incomplete. Settlement had faltered, beaten back by distance, a challenging climate and inhospitable terrain. As the Queensland squatters swept north, Governor Bowen had exulted and seen the advance as an extension of the Empire. A hundred years later, in 1959, Queensland commemorated its centenary with the publication of a celebratory volume entitled *Triumph in the Tropics*.[19] But by then the forces of decolonisation were sweeping the world. The Empire that Bowen knew was in the final stages of disintegration. Right across the north of the continent there was a vigorous Aboriginal resurgence. From the 1960s, demographic rebound and political activism combined to stimulate increasingly urgent demands for land rights and for recognition of the legitimate claims to ancestral homelands. Native title has now been acquired over vast areas of the tropical north, and many small communities have returned to once abandoned but still cherished locations.

But what about sovereignty? Many questions await answers. Did the First Nations exercise it over their bounded territories? Was it lost when the British annexed the various parts of the continent or did it survive as James Stephen clearly thought almost 200 years ago? Have aspects of sovereignty survived along with elements of customary law? Is there still a right to self-determination? If land title can be retrieved, can other rights be reclaimed in like manner? The gap between what the men and women of the First Nations believe and what the 'whitefella' law determines will continue to widen. It was some time ago now that an elder of the Yawuru Nation set down his views on the question of Aboriginal sovereignty:

> It's time our Aboriginal lawyers – so called Aboriginal leaders came to the East and West Kimberleys so that we the Elders of the Independent Nations can teach them of our system of governance, sovereignty.
>
> Even today we still respect each nation Sovereignty over their specific country, we are all independent of outside authority.
>
> It has been our system of governance since time immemorial ... Each nation governed within their territorial borders. Our system was harsh but just ... Internal sovereignty is paramount power over all action within. The anthropologist[s] of yesteryear have done us great injustice by not recording our system of justice, and that we were not one nation.[20]

It is hard to imagine a more effective rejection of traditional Western legal doctrine. The only viable riposte is to assert that Indigenous sovereignty was extinguished in apocalyptic moments in 1788, 1824 and 1829 when the British annexed the three large pieces of the continent. This view may prevail when it comes to external sovereignty, but it simply will not do where Indigenous rights are concerned. The only realistic alternative is the proposition that sovereignty, like land ownership, was subverted in a piecemeal fashion over a great many years. If that is the central story, it leaves wide open the alternative view that in many parts of the continent the momentum of the invasion stalled, leaving Indigenous society still in occupation of its traditional lands and continuing to exercise its ancient sovereignty.

5

AUSTRALIA AND
THE LAW OF NATIONS

In the Uluru Statement the Aboriginal delegates declared that the 'Aboriginal and Torres Strait Islander tribes were the first sovereign nations of the Australian continent' and they 'possessed it under our own laws and customs'. More to the point it had 'never been ceded or extinguished and co-exists with the sovereignty of the Crown'. It was perhaps the most important and potentially contentious aspect of the State- ment from the Heart. But can this be true? Or perhaps more to the point is there any support for it in either international or domestic law? This is not a simple question and there are no easy answers. International law provides more support for the statement than do contemporary interpretations in Australian law. We should begin with MF Lindley's classic 1926 study *The Acquisition and Government of Backward Territory in International Law.*

When addressing the question of whether Indigenous people such as the Aboriginal Australians could be consid- ered to have exercised sovereignty 'under the law of nations', Lindley explained that answers varied widely and changed over time. But the many commentators could be grouped into three, more or less, definite schools. They were:

1   'Those who regard backward races as possessing a title
     to the sovereignty over the territory they inhabit which
     is good as against more highly civilized peoples.'
2   'Those who admit such a title in the natives, but only
     with restrictions or under conditions.'
3   'Those who do not consider that the natives possess
     rights of such a nature as to be a bar to the assumption of
     sovereignty over them by more highly civilized people.'

Lindley judged that the collective weight of opinion favoured
his first group, writing that 'Comparing these three schools
of thought, we see that, extending over some three and a half
centuries, there has been a persistent preponderance of juristic
opinion in favour of the proposition that lands in the possession of any backward peoples who are politically organized
ought not be regarded as if they belonged to no one.'[1]

There is clearly more support in international law for the
Uluru Statement than many Australians likely imagine. The
nation's jurisprudence has been dominated by Lindley's third
school of thought and overwhelmed by the doctrine of *terra
nullius*. But if we return to the writing of international jurists
over 'three and a half centuries', it will be necessary to consider
how sovereignty was conceptualised, how it related to the control of territory, and what cultural, social and political characteristics were required for it to be recognised and respected.

Political independence was one of the essential elements
for sovereignty and was stressed by many writers. In the
17th century, German legal scholar Samuel Rachel argued in
De Jure Naturae that 'one state has no authority over another,

nor one free people over another; nor is one of them under liability to another of them, and much less are several free peoples and States subordinate to some one power – but each of them has its own [independence] and [self-rule]'.[2]

Independence clearly depended on the will and the ability to exclude others from the sovereign homeland. In *A Methodical System of Universal Law* of 1773, JG Heineccius observed that 'dominion consists solely in the faculty of excluding others from the use of a thing'.[3] Every nation that governed itself, Emmerich de Vattel wrote in 1758, 'under whatever form, and which does not depend on any other Nation is a *sovereign State*'.[4] In his *Elements of International Law* published in 1836, Henry Wheaton declared that a sovereign state was generally defined 'to be any nation or people, whatever may be the form of its internal constitution, which governs itself independently of foreign powers'.[5] There is abundant evidence to establish that Australia's First Nations, while small, preserved their independence and defended their boundaries against interlopers. And it is likely they did this over long periods of time. Their great linguistic diversity allows for no other conclusion.

But were they too small to be regarded as sovereign states? There is no ready answer to this question. The international jurists did consider the matter but provided no precise figure as to the size required for the exercise of sovereign authority. In 1660, Samuel von Pufendorf thought it all depended on the comparative size of contiguous states. The 'just size of a state', he declared, 'should be measured by the strength of its neighbours'.[6] Eighteenth-century writers were more specific about the size and strength of states. De Vattel argued that nations should be regarded as though they were 'so many free persons' living in a state of nature and who were by nature equal, holding the same obligations and the 'same rights'. Strength or weakness counted for nothing. 'A dwarf is as much a man as a giant is', he observed, 'a small Republic no less a sovereign State than the most powerful kingdom.'[7] De Vattel's mentor, Christian Wolff, pursued a similar line of argument in his *Law of Nations*. It was not the number of men coming together that made a nation but 'the bond by which individuals are united' and that was 'nothing else than the obligation by which they are bound to one another'. Therefore just as the tallest man is no more a man than a dwarf, so also a nation 'however small, is no less a nation than the greatest nation'. In fact, the moral equality of nations had 'no relation to the number of men of which they are composed'.[8] John Austin, the eminent 19th-century British jurist, looked at the same question in his *Lectures on Jurisprudence*:

> In order that an independent society may form a society political, it must not fall short of a *number* which may be called considerable.
>
> The lowest possible number which will satisfy that vague condition cannot be fixed precisely. But, looking at many of the communities which commonly are considered and treated as independent political societies, we must infer that an independent society may form a society political, although the number of its members exceed not a few thousands, or exceed not a few hundreds.[9]

Size was one thing, culture was another matter altogether. What characteristics were required for a nation to be considered as capable of exercising sovereignty that could be recognised by the established nations of the world? Sixteenth-century Spain was the first of the European nations to debate the status of the Indigenous Americans incorporated in their vast South American empire. In 1532, the jurist Francisco de Vitoria decided that the Indians had 'true dominion in both public and private matters, just like Christians ...' Even if it was conceded that they were 'as inept and stupid as is alleged', dominion could not 'be denied to them'.[10] Hugo Grotius, recognised as the founder of European international law, discussed the question of the rights of non-Christians in 1609 in his book *The Freedom of the Seas*. Surely it is a heresy, he declared,

> to believe that infidels are not masters of their own
> property; consequently, to take from them their possessions
> on account of their religious beliefs is no less theft and
> robbery than it would be in the case of Christians ...
> Nor are the East Indians stupid and unthinking; on the
> contrary they are intelligent and shrewd so that the pretext
> for subduing them on the ground of their character could
> not be sustained. Such a pretext on its very face is an
> injustice ... And now that well known pretext of forcing
> nations into a higher state of civilization against their
> will ... is considered by all theologians ... to be unjust
> and unholy. They [heathens and infidels] are not to be
> deprived of sovereignty over their possessions because of

their unbelief, since sovereignty is a matter of positive law,
and unbelief a matter of divine law ... In fact I know of
no law against such unbelievers as regards their temporal
possessions. Against them no King, no Emperor, not even
the Roman Church can declare war for the purpose of
occupying their lands, or of subjecting them to temporal
sway.[11]

These cultural arguments of Grotius are pertinent to
the legal and moral justification associated with the British
annexation of Australia and, at the very least, the implicit
assumption that 'civilised' nations could legitimately seize the
property and usurp the sovereignty of 'savage' and 'barbarous'
peoples. And the ideas propounded in the early 17th century
did not disappear from international law in the 18th. Christian
Wolff, considered at the time the greatest jurist of the age, trod
the same path as Grotius. He argued that while it was appropriate for 'learned and cultivated' nations to do whatever they
could to assist 'barbarous and uncultivated' ones, it could not
be done forcibly, for

if any nation wishes to promote the perfection of another,
it cannot compel it to allow that to be done; if some
barbarous and uncultivated nation is unwilling to accept
aid offered to it by another in removing its barbarism
and rendering its manners more cultivated, it cannot
be compelled to accept such aid ... Barbarism and
uncultivated manners give you no right against a nation ...
Therefore a war is unjust which is begun on this pretext.[12]

Another question of sovereignty that was addressed by international jurists was whether tribal communities engaged in hunting and herding could be considered as political societies with laws and customs of an appropriate kind. Wheaton outlined the way a state is distinguished from an 'unsettled horde of wandering savages not yet formed into civil society'.[13] De Vattel thought that a nation or a state was 'a political body, a society of men who have united together and combined their forces in order to procure their mutual welfare and security'.[14] Wolff too distinguished between a nation and a group of unrelated families. So were the Australian tribes 'unsettled hordes' or civil societies according to European thinking in the late 18th and early 19th centuries? What was the essential difference?

Wheaton argued that the legal idea of a state necessarily implied the 'habitual obedience of its members to those persons in whom the superiority is vested'.[15] Many other jurists agreed. Authority, order and obedience were seen as the critical measures of a political society. English jurist Jeremy Bentham argued in 1776 that the difference between the state of nature and a political society lay 'in the *habit of obedience*'.[16] William Blackstone before him observed that obedience was not to be understood as a 'transient sudden order from a superior, to or concerning a particular person' but rather something that was 'permanent, uniform and universal'. Unless there was some authority 'whose commands and decisions all the members are bound to obey' the community in question 'would still remain as in a state of nature, without any judge upon earth to define their several rights, and redress their several wrongs'.[17]

Austin was another jurist who believed that the fundamental difference between political and natural societies was whether 'the generality' of its members 'be in the habit of obedience'. In a natural society, obedience was 'rendered by so few of the members' that a more general obedience was 'unfrequent and broken'. In a political society, on the other hand, the bulk of the population were in 'a habit of obedience or submission to a determinate and common superior: let that common superior be a certain individual person, or a certain body or aggregate of individual persons'. Austin directed his attention specifically to the 'case of tribes such as those who live by hunting or fishing in the woods or on the coast of New Holland' and those tribes of Native Americans who 'range the unsettled parts of the North American continent'. He wondered if they had sufficient cohesion to be considered independent political societies because the bonds connecting them were 'too slight to say that they render habitual obedience to any certain superior'. But if, on the contrary, the tribal groups met the conditions of obedience to an established set of laws or customs, they must be considered to be a 'congeries of independent political communities ... however small'. They had 'all the marks of independent political societies except size'.[18]

How was this relevant to Australia? When the British arrived they knew almost nothing about the inner dynamics of Aboriginal society. In his account of the first years in Sydney Watkin Tench commented in 1789 that: 'It would be trespassing on the reader's indulgence were I to impose on him an account of any civil regulations, or ordinances, which may possibly exist among these people. I declare to him, that

I knew not of any … Whether any law exists among them for the punishment of offences committed against society … I will not positively affirm.'[19] The understanding of Indigenous law and custom evolved slowly, but by the 1840s explorers like George Grey, Edward Eyre and Paul de Strzelecki had published books that provided readers with the first serious assessment of the situation. The three men were impressed not by the absence or weakness of customary laws but their strength and durability. Strzelecki believed that, what he called 'traditionary customs' were as 'rigorously adhered to as amongst civilized nations'.[20] Eyre went further, arguing that 'Through custom's irresistible sway has been forged the chains that bind in iron fetters a people, who might otherwise be said to be without government or restraint.'[21] Grey was even more impressed with the 'tenacity and undeviating strictness' of customary law, which was 'fixed in the minds of the people as sacred and unalterable'. They were not free but 'in reality subjected to complex laws', which deprived them of 'all free agency of thought'.[22] Ethnography of the following hundred years broadly confirmed these early insights. Aboriginal peoples clearly had 'the habit of obedience'.

Another test of sovereignty traditionally applied to hunters and herders was whether they were actually in possession of a defined piece of territory. Without acknowledged territory there could be no sovereignty. There needed to be what Wheaton called 'a fixed abode, and determined territory belonging to the people by whom it is occupied'.[23] To what extent was this relevant to Australia? We have seen above that it did not take long for the officers of the First Fleet to realise that the Aboriginal bands close to Sydney had clearly defined territories, and as more people gained experience in the hinterland this assessment was confirmed. Missionaries and official government protectors reported that the different tribes functioned like small but independent nations. Edward Parker, a protector of Aborigines at Port Phillip in the 1840s, explained that

> I found on my first investigations into the character of these people, that the country was occupied by a number of petty nations, easily distinguished from each other by their having a distinct dialect or language as well as by other peculiarities. Each occupied its own portion of country and so, as far as I could learn, never intruded into each other's territory, except when engaged in hostilities, or invited by regularly appointed messengers.[24]

Parker's colleague James Dredge concluded similarly that Aboriginal Australia was 'divided into a number of petty states' which, whether 'large or small, weak or powerful', were 'entirely distinct from each other' as related to 'the territory they inhabit, and the control and management of their own affairs'.[25] In Tasmania the land commissioner Roderic O'Connor found in the 1820s that the tribes were 'various', were 'in every direction in the Island' and composed 'as it were of so many different nations'.[26] A generation later the Victorian pioneer Edward Curr published a major work summing up much of the ethnographic information that had accumulated over the century since the start of the invasion.

He explained that the whole of Australia was 'parcelled out' among the tribes 'probably many centuries back' and before the intrusion of the Europeans; 'each tribe held its territory ... against all intruders'.[27]

And so, if we bring together the international jurisprudence of the generations both immediately before and then after 1788 with the great body of ethnographic information gathered by interested settlers, it is clear that the small Aboriginal nations exercised sovereignty over their traditional homelands. But shortly after Curr's four volumes were published in Melbourne, the Privy Council in London considered an Australian case relating to a property dispute, and in doing so made a major statement about the settlement of Australia. There was, Lord Watson declared in 1889,

> a great difference between the case of a Colony acquired by conquest or cession, in which there is an established system of law, and that of a Colony which consists of a tract of territory practically unoccupied, without settled inhabitants or settled law, at the time when it was peacefully annexed to the British dominions. The Colony of New South Wales belongs to the latter class.[28]

Lord Watson's law was clearly impervious to the knowledge of Aboriginal society that had been accumulated for a hundred years, or to the jurisprudence I have summarised to this point. It is doubtful if he or his colleagues knew much about Australia or had any interest in finding out about it. But if they cast an eye on the decisions of the colonial courts, they would have come across the leading case of *R v Murrell* heard in the New South Wales Supreme Court in 1836. Like *Cooper v Stuart* (see chapter 1), it cast a very long shadow. It needs considerable attention.

The case concerned Jack Congo Murrell, who was brought before the Supreme Court on a charge of murder in February 1836. With a relative George Bummary, he had killed two other Aboriginal men at Windsor in what was apparently a revenge attack in retribution for the earlier killing of a kinsman. At the time there was some legal uncertainty about whether the courts should deal with crimes committed among the Indigenous people, and in Murrell's defence it was argued that the Aboriginal peoples had laws and customs of their own that should be considered in any settlement of the case. This proposition was dismissed by Justice William Burton, with his fellow judges Francis Forbes and James Dowling concurring. In doing so, Burton considered the legal principles underpinning the establishment of New South Wales and the resulting status of the Aboriginal peoples, arguing that 'although it might be granted that on the first taking possession of the Colony, the Aborigines were entitled to be recognized as free and independent, yet they were not in such a position with regard to strength as to be considered free and independent tribes'.[29]

What is more, they 'had no sovereignty', the judgment said, because they had not attained to such a position 'in point of numbers and civilization' and to such a form of government and laws 'as to be entitled to be recognized as so many sovereign states governed by laws of their own'.[30] Burton considered the question in his case notes as well as in his published judgment. They allow a closer examination of his reasoning. 'Yet I deny', he argued,

> that these tribes are entitled to be considered as so many Sovereign or Independent Tribes in as much as that depends not only on their independence of any foreign control but having also attained to such a situation in point of numbers and civilization as a nation and to such a settled form of government and such settled laws that civilized Nations are bound to know and respect them.[31]

Another reason Burton found to disregard Aboriginal rights was that although Aboriginal peoples appeared to have customary laws they were founded entirely upon principles of the most 'indiscriminating notions of revenge'. They could not be considered to be ancient laws of the country that could be allowed to survive. They were to be regarded 'only in the light of lewd practices' similar to the 'laws of the Wild Irish'. The Common Law should be imposed on them in all situations. It was, Burton declared, 'a mild and merciful conquest thus to subdue them'.[32]

Burton's judgment in *R v Murrell* was very influential. With it, the leading court in the Australian colonies reaffirmed the decision that the legal situation of the Aboriginal peoples had not changed since the formal annexation of New South Wales in 1788. They had no sovereignty. Nor did they have land law or tenure. Britain acquired sovereignty neither by conquest nor by cession. It was an original, not a derived sovereignty. This interpretation was stamped deeply into Australian law and was reaffirmed on many later occasions. In the case *R v Wedge* in New South Wales in 1976, Justice Arthur Rath rejected the proposition that Aboriginal people were not subject to Australian law. He referred to *R v Murrell*, declaring that Burton's arguments were 'as valid today as they were when judgment was given on 19/2/1836'.[33]

But the intellectual support for Rath's interpretation was falling away. It was after all an era of worldwide decolonisation and the drafting of charters of human rights. International law moved in sympathy. A few months before the decision in *R v Wedge* was handed down, the International Court of Justice at The Hague dealt a deathblow to the idea of *terra nullius* even if it was little noticed in Australia at the time. The case involved a territorial dispute between Spain, Mauritania and Morocco about the legal status of the Western Sahara still known as the Spanish Sahara. Late in 1974, the General Assembly of the United Nations asked the court for an opinion on the competing claims.

Much turned on the legitimacy of the Spanish annexation in 1884. It depended, as did the British claim over Australia, on the assertion that the nomadic tribes of the territory did not exercise sovereignty over the land they occupied, which was a *terra nullius* and as a result Spain acquired an original, not a derived sovereignty. If any Australians were following the proceedings, it all would have sounded very familiar. The first question the court was asked to determine was the current legal standing of *terra nullius*. The fifteen judges gave a unanimous judgment: territories inhabited by people having a social and political organisation were not regarded as *terra nullius*. Spain either had a title by cession or no title at all. The effect of the judgment was to determine that occupation of territory was only open as regards 'uninhabited territories or territories inhabited only by a number of individuals not constituting a social or political aggregation'. And a more critical point is that while the decision reflected modern sensibilities, it referred back to the 18th century, providing 'posthumous rehabilitation of the classic authors of international law'.[34]

Clearly the doctrine of the 'settled colony' is still deeply entrenched in Australian law. It is necessarily associated with the concept of *terra nullius*. The two ideas cannot be prised apart. One is totally dependent on the other. The sovereignty of the Australian state is compromised because it is premised on the assumption that the First Nations were too primitive to have exercised what the Uluru Statement calls their 'ancient sovereignty'. As a result, the Australian courts have summarily dismissed any challenges to the legal status quo and have given no support whatsoever to the idea that there may be some form of surviving, subsidiary, Indigenous sovereignty. At the same time, the judges have refused to give any legitimacy to the idea that Australian First Nations ever were, or ever can be, accorded the status of 'domestic dependent nations' in the North American manner.

Aboriginal litigants went before both state and federal courts to challenge Australian sovereignty in a number of cases between 1976 and 1994. The arguments differed, the decisions were uniform. In 1979 Paul Coe sought to sue the Commonwealth of Australia on behalf of the Aboriginal community and nation of Australia. He claimed that both Cook in 1770 and Phillip in 1788 had wrongly proclaimed sovereignty and dominion over eastern Australia. He argued that from time immemorial before 1770 the Aboriginal nation had enjoyed exclusive sovereignty over the whole continent. Some of the Aboriginal people still exercised those rights. In essence, Coe's case foreshadowed the propositions of the Uluru Statement. But the High Court would have none of it, decisively rejecting Coe's claim. Justice Kenneth Jacobs determined that the questions at issue were not matters of domestic law but of the law of nations. In fact they were not 'cognisable in a court exercising jurisdiction under that sovereignty which is sought to be challenged'. Justice Harry Gibbs was even more dismissive, observing that 'The contention that there is in Australia an aboriginal nation exercising sovereignty, even of a limited kind, is quite impossible in law to maintain.'[35] Subsequent cases received the same decisive rejection.

The *Mabo* case of 1992 produced a quite different result. As is now widely understood the High Court, in a six to one decision, overturned the assertion of Lord Watson in 1889 that at the time of annexation there was no land law or tenure in Australia. Aboriginal native title could be recognised in Australian courts and in many places had not been extinguished. It was indeed a jurisprudential revolution and was recognised as such. So one part of *terra nullius* had been abandoned. But property was one thing; sovereignty quite another. Mabo's team did not seek to question the legitimacy of the annexation of the Murray Islands in 1879, and the court made it quite clear that sovereignty was not to be questioned. The reasons for this require closer examination. We should begin with a consideration of the views of Eddie Mabo himself.

His crusade began when he realised that he had no title to his family's land on Murray (Meer) Island in the Torres Strait even though it was clearly marked and used for growing crops, was acknowledged by island custom and had been occupied by the extended family for generations. It was an astonishing revelation that all the land on Murray and Darnley (Erub) Islands was owned by the Crown. His reaction was not surprising. It dramatically illustrated the extraordinary usurpation implicit in the idea of a settled colony at the heart of Australian law. To lose land as a result of conquest or following on from negotiation with clan leaders would have been understandable, if still unacceptable. But to have traditional land tenure confiscated a hundred years ago by white men who had never actually been on the islands was enough to strain credulity. It was very likely that no European had ever seen or walked on the land in question. The bigger problem was how generations of Australians could have thought such expropriation reasonable, honourable or legitimate.

Mabo was equally concerned with the question of sovereignty. He had grown up with almost no experience of Australian society. For many years the Murray Islanders were not allowed to live on, or even visit, mainland Australia. Apart from one school teacher no 'whitefellas' resided permanently on Murray Island. The Islanders ran their domestic affairs according to their own customs and ways of doing things. They managed and crewed their own ships. But their autonomy notwithstanding they were still subject to Queensland law and the often arbitrary decisions made by state government bureaucrats who could exile so-called troublemakers to places like Palm Island for indefinite periods.

And when Eddie had moved to Townsville in the 1960s the same officials were able to prevent him from returning to his island even for his father's funeral. The political control exercised by a government situated almost 2000 kilometres away seemed as arbitrary and unacceptable as the expropriation of land. And once he had come to the mainland he quickly became aware of what was happening in the wider world as decolonisation reached its climax. Papua New Guinea gained its independence in 1975. Port Moresby was both culturally and geographically closer to Murray Island than Brisbane. And then in 1979 Norfolk Island was granted self-government. The relevance of this development was obvious to Torres Strait Islanders.

Eddie wanted to be able to challenge both the expropriation of property and the imposition of sovereignty, but was persuaded by his legal team to concentrate on land ownership. It was good advice. If he had lived to read the judgment he would have appreciated it. In the four separate judgments, the bench explained why the annexation of 1879 could not be questioned. Any challenge faced a series of legal hurdles. Justices William Deane and Mary Gaudron observed that 'it must be accepted in this Court' that the original claim of sovereignty in 1788 'validly established a "settled" British Colony'.[36] Referring to Murray Island, their colleague Justice Daryl Dawson remarked that 'The annexation of the Murray Islands is not now questioned. It was an act of state by which the Crown in right of the Colony of Queensland exerted sovereignty over the islands. Whatever the justification for the acquisition of territory by this means … there can be no doubt that it was, and remains, legally effective.'[37]

The court followed established law in considering the question of sovereignty, arguing that the Crown, while acting outside Britain itself and on the international stage, exercised prerogative powers that were beyond the reach of domestic or municipal courts as they are termed. These principles were reaffirmed in Australia by the High Court in the so-called *Seas and Submerged Lands Case* in 1975. Justice Gibbs argued that the acquisition of territory by a sovereign state for the first time was 'an act of state which cannot be challenged, controlled or interfered with by the Courts of the State'.[38] Justice Gerard Brennan followed suit in Mabo, explaining that the law was such that it precluded any contest between the executive and judicial branches of government as to whether a territory was or was not within the 'Queen's Domain'. Such questions were 'not justiciable in the municipal courts'.[39] What was more any doubt about the claims of sovereignty, any questioning of the settled colony doctrine would threaten to 'fracture the skeleton of principle which gives the body of our law its shape and internal consistency'.[40]

The Australian courts have no doubt followed sound legal doctrine in their judgments about sovereignty. But can they really expect that this will encourage respect for the law itself? Are we really constrained in our legal thinking by the decisions made in London in 1786 when Phillip received his commission, and embodied in the proclamations he read in Sydney in February 1788, as we have seen above? Is the judicial system so rigid that the founding doctrine cannot be challenged? The implication is that Australia judicially is still a colony of Great Britain still awaiting the coming of decolonisation. But above all, why should the First Nations respect laws that are premised on the notion that their ancestors were wandering savages? Why would they feel any affection for legal ideas that were a direct cause of profound loss and suffering? More specifically, why would Mabo have accepted the decision that sanctioned the annexation carried out by the Queensland government in 1879? Murray Island had none of the characteristics of a *terra nullius* and that was obvious at the time. And the Queensland government had a shocking international reputation as a result of its treatment of Aboriginal peoples and scandals regarding the Pacific Island labour trade. Five years after the annexation of the Murray Islands, Queensland declared sovereignty over Papua. William Gladstone's British Liberal government rescinded the claim because Queensland had proved itself incapable of dealing justly towards Indigenous people. It is not at all clear how this action fitted in with legal doctrine embraced by the Australian High Court a hundred years later. How was the intercession of the Crown 'in right of the colony of Queensland' simply dismissed by the British government? If the British government could overturn the claim of sovereignty over Papua in 1884, why couldn't the Australian governments similarly overturn the claim over Murray Island five years before?

We have seen that in his judgment in *Coe v Commonwealth*, Justice Jacobs determined that questions about sovereignty were not matters of domestic laws but of the 'law of nations'. If that is true, advocates of the First Nations may have to begin the task of seeking a settlement in the International Court of Justice. It will be a fight that Eddie Mabo would have relished.

6

'TREATY YEH, TREATY NOW'

When Yothu Yindi's now famous song 'Treaty' went to the top of the charts in 1991 it was almost certainly the first time that many listeners had heard of the campaign for the negotiation of a treaty between the Australian state and the First Nations. The subject had been periodically discussed in the mainstream media during the previous decade, but there was little understanding of the matter among the general public. It was, after all, a novel idea, and a common response at the time was to insist that while treaties were signed with other sovereign states, they could not be made with minority groups within the one country. The idea seemed somewhat subversive and likely to divide the nation. People had heard of New Zealand's Treaty of Waitangi, but there was little awareness of the long tradition of treaty-making in North America, even within the legal profession. Almost no one appreciated that the absence of treaties in Australia had been noticed in the earliest colonial years, or that Jeremy Bentham had written about the matter 200 years before 'Treaty' was composed and sung.

Bentham's prediction about the consequences of proceeding with the colonial project without the required legal instruments became apparent in Tasmania in the 1820s. Governor

George Arthur was one of Britain's most able colonial governors and he had an unusually long term of twelve years in Tasmania. Half of that time was overshadowed by violent frontier war. As he reflected on his experience he became convinced that much of the trouble stemmed from the fact that there had been no treaties. He believed that they should have been negotiated at the very beginning of settlement in order to control the colonists. He was quite certain that the local nations would have been able to clearly understand the meaning and purpose of such documents. Perhaps more to the point was that George Augustus Robinson had negotiated a settlement that brought the war to an end. It was a peace treaty in all but name. The British did not honour the terms of the treaty that Robinson clearly set out in his journal. But the Aboriginal peoples were quite certain that they had an agreement with 'the old governor'. And legally this matters. Both the common law and international law provide support to the Indigenous interpretation.

The United Nations Declaration on the Rights of Indigenous People was adopted by the General Assembly in September 2007 and ratified by Australia in 2009. Among its many provisions is a little noticed section about historic treaties. It reads: 'Indigenous Peoples have the right to the recognition, observance and enforcement of Treaties, Agreements and other Constructive Arrangements concluded with States or their successors and to have States honour and respect such Treaties, Agreements and other Constructive Arrangements.'[1]

The second support for the continuing viability of historical agreements comes from the common law as interpreted by the Canadian Supreme Court in the landmark 1990 case *R v Sioui*. The matter in dispute was the right of the four Sioui brothers to camp in a national park that had been created in 1895 in their traditional Huron homeland. The case made its way over seven years from the provincial courts in Quebec to the Supreme Court. The brothers' defence was that their ancestors had reached an agreement in 1760 with the military commander of the region, General James Murray, that recognised their right to use the land in question for ceremonial purposes. The Supreme Court in a unanimous judgment accepted the argument and overturned the brothers' prior convictions.

R v Sioui was recognised at the time as an authoritative interpretation of how the courts must approach treaties negotiated between the First Nations and the Crown. How old the agreement was did not matter. Rights guaranteed in treaties or agreements remained valid unless the descendants themselves relinquished them. Such agreements should be liberally construed and, where uncertainties in the law existed, interpreted in a manner that favoured First Nations. Even more interesting was the declaration that treaties and agreements must be understood from the perspective of the First Nations. When considering whether historical agreements were, in fact treaties 'a liberal and generous attitude, heedful of historical fact', must be employed. The critical point was whether the Indigenous Canadians had reason to believe that an agreement amounted to a treaty. The threshold issue determining whether or not a document was a treaty was to answer the question of the capacity of the parties involved. 'The question of capacity must be seen from the point of view of the Indians at the time, and the Court must ask whether it was reasonable for them to have assumed that the other party they were dealing with had the authority to enter into a valid treaty with them.'[2]

There is no doubt that George Augustus Robinson was acting with the authority bestowed on him by the governor and told everyone, Aboriginal and European alike, that he was engaged in what was, in effect, a diplomatic mission. It was entirely reasonable for the Aboriginal peoples to have a belief that they were dealing with a person who had the authority to enter into a valid treaty. What they didn't understand was the need to ask for a written agreement. Their own internal politics was conducted by way of binding verbal understandings. Had they demanded a written document they would very likely have received one. The terms of the agreement were not honoured by the colonial government. The colonists soon forgot that their government had negotiated what was, in effect, a treaty in their name. It took much longer for it to fade in the memory of the survivors of war, exile and illness. But one thing is clear. While we cannot precisely date the moment when the Tasmanian war began we know exactly when it ended. It was Saturday 7 January 1832, when the leaders of the Big River and Oyster Bay nations marched into Hobart for a conference with Governor Arthur.

The Australian-born pioneer John Batman may not have been in Hobart on that day, but he would certainly have participated in conversations among Tasmanian settlers about treaties with the Aboriginal peoples and, for that matter, about the opportunities that beckoned on the far side of Bass Strait. As is well known, Batman led a party of Tasmanians to Port Phillip in June 1835 and negotiated access to a large area of land between the present sites of Melbourne and Geelong. Batman called the agreement a treaty and it is still largely known by that name. This is misleading in several ways. There is no way whatsoever that a private subject of the Crown could negotiate a treaty. Declaration of war, negotiation of peace and treaty-making are powers reserved for the Crown and jealously preserved. That was so then. It is so now. Unlike Robinson, Batman had no delegated authority whatsoever. He had negotiated a private arrangement and no more than that. So the idea that what Batman did was unique is quite misconceived. Private agreements were negotiated between frontiersmen and resident bands many times, all over the country. The absence of overarching treaties made this both inevitable and essential. Most of them have been lost to the historical record. There has been little attempt to give them the scholarly attention they clearly deserve. But without some understanding of them, our picture of the relations between First Nations and frontiersmen is manifestly distorted.

The concentration in a generation of scholarship on white violence has been both understandable and necessary. It was the most effective way to shatter the great Australian silence. But it leaves us with a seriously depleted picture of the complex nature of frontier history. The meeting of frontiersmen and First Nations did, in many cases, result in violent conflict. But how soon it began and how long it lasted was variable and depended on many things. Terrain was clearly important, but so too was the inclination of both sides. What is often missed is that what we are dealing with are situations where politics and diplomacy were as important as physical force. Negotiation superseded bloodshed in some places. A minority of frontiersmen were able to come to terms with local bands. When these arrangements were reported, the emphasis was usually on the good will of the squatter. But there may have been an equally important Indigenous desire for a negotiated settlement. The bands that had to deal with the unprecedented challenge of the arrival of the first permanent party of settlers would have been aware of the encroaching wave and had probably known for months or even years that the white men were coming. They may have made surreptitious journeys of discovery to find out as much as possible about the invaders, to gather intelligence about their behaviour and what fate had befallen neighbouring nations. They would have heard long before about white men's guns and their large exotic animals. We can presume there were many discussions about what tactics should be adopted. This helps us understand the variety of the Indigenous response, the choices that were made. Immediate confrontation did occur, but it was not necessarily the most common reaction. Avoidance and wary surveillance were often adopted, and were an easy option given the size of national territory and the small number of European interlopers. In places young women were sent forward on what were essentially diplomatic missions. The most ambitious and risky venture was to endeavour to incorporate the white men into the web of local kinship.

But in those places where peaceful transitions were arranged, it is likely that what was needed was at least latent good will on both sides but also an uneasy awareness of impending danger. There seem to have been some common characteristics of successful negotiations, including under-standings about access to water, and about hunting parties avoiding sheep and cattle. In exchange, animals were regularly slaughtered and given to the local band in return for a promise not to spear them out on the range. Supply of tobacco, tea and sugar soon became a major contributor to successful negoti-ation. But an even more significant factor was the provision of young men, who quickly acquired the new skills that, when added to traditional bushcraft, made them valuable additions to any station's workforce. Young women were provided to be trained in domestic work and to provide sexual comfort. It was often done with reluctance but with an understanding that if not mutually arranged the women would be taken by force. But a frequent underlying consideration was that with a negotiated arrangement the station in question became a rel-atively secure haven away from ambient violence. The 'white boss' became a defender of 'his' blacks, even able at times to protect them from violent neighbours and marauding native police patrols.

Violence was the most common result of the arrival of the 'whitefellas', but it came to an end everywhere sooner or later. This became apparent when the survivors of the conflict 'came in' to stations, mining camps and small rudimentary towns. 'Coming in' has received far less attention than the outbreak of conflict. Who actually initiated the move is often difficult to tell. It was possibly an Indigenous decision as often as a 'white-fella' one. It was often fraught and dangerous. But at some point the cost of conflict became too great to be sustained. This was obviously the case from the Aboriginal point of view. Survival itself was in the balance. But the Europeans themselves had no particular interest in perpetual conflict. It was expensive. It drove up the cost of labour and was the source of an aching anxiety that took its toll. It was hard to look forward to a normal life while living in an armed camp. Some frontiersmen seemed to take pleasure in killing and the frisson of conflict. But most didn't. And above all the local tribespeople were a promising source of desperately needed labour.

This was an urgent consideration everywhere in northern Australia. There were no convicts. White labour was scarce, expensive and unreliable. And by the second half of the 19th century, the value of Aboriginal labour was well known and had been illustrated by generally acknowledged examples stretching back for several generations. So the frequent references to the colonists' genocidal intent are wide of the mark. The pastoralists did not want an empty land but one with a constant ready supply of Aboriginal labour and sexual partners. They did not want dead blacks but biddable and submissive servants; men and women who were committed to their country, would not wander away and would cost very little. Indeed, the northern pastoral industry was totally dependent on Aboriginal labour and remained so until the middle of the 20th century.

What are we to make of these hundreds of local agreements? Clearly the frontiersmen and their successors used actual violence, the threat of violence or even its latent possibility to gain control of vast areas of the tropical savannah and thus were able to establish a viable, if constantly challenged, pastoral industry. They were not treaties and were achieved with little involvement of the governments of Queensland, South Australia and Western Australia. The frontier police forces were small and understaffed, given the vast areas for which they were responsible. But they provided the force to keep what can legitimately be called the post-war settlement in place. But larger considerations press forward. They illustrate the validity of what George Arthur had come to realise many years before and hundreds of kilometres away in the far south. Treaties could have been made with the First Nations, whose leaders would have fully understood what was at stake and would have been willing to negotiate settlements. With the power of the state employed to facilitate agreements, how different frontier history might have been. Arthur thought one of the advantages of having a treaty was that it would have given him a legal framework that would enable him to control the behaviour of the settlers.

The Colonial Office clearly had similar ideas in mind when, in 1848, it imposed pastoral leases on the Australian colonies a few years before they gained their power of internal self-government. What potential authority they contained! Here was the legal structure to oversee new settlements all over the continent. The whole of northern Australia could have been settled with government supervision enforcing acceptance of the Aboriginal peoples' right to remain on their ancestral land. It could so easily have established the principle that refusal to accept these legal requirements would lead to forfeiture of the lease. The three governments were able to administer the vast expansion of settlement, to survey the runs and issue appropriate legal documents. How different it all might have been if they had accepted their responsibility to the First Nations. If Queensland, for instance, had put as much effort into establishing a service to oversee local agreements and enforce the reality of shared use rights instead of a paramilitary force to drive Aboriginal peoples off their land, hundreds of lives might have been saved. Local agreements were eventually arranged everywhere sooner or later. How much fairer they might have been if supervised and their terms enforced by the government. Expansion into northern Australia might have ended up with a series of treaties.

Australians are slow to relate their history to other, comparable countries. But the conquest on the vast northern rangelands in the second half of the 19th century was contemporaneous with the wars in Argentina and Chile to gain complete control of the grasslands of Patagonia and the settlement of the prairies in the United States and Canada. In all cases, Indigenous societies were being rapidly dispossessed, usually, but not always, violently. In Argentina and Chile, the armed forces carried out formal campaigns that continue to be commemorated in national storytelling. The same is true with the prolonged conflict between the United States cavalry and the Plains American Indians. All three countries recognise the conflict as warfare. In each place, the forces of the colonial states were armed with the greatly improved weapons used right across northern Australia.

The Canadian case is very different. The new Confederation gained full control of the vast prairies from the Great

Lakes to the Rockies by the means of treaties negotiated by the newly formed North-West Mounted Police. Seven treaties were signed between 1871 and 1877 covering the prairies, and then a second group of four relating to areas further north between 1899 and 1921. Each treaty was different, but there were common features. The Indigenous Canadians ceded control over large areas of their traditional lands to make way for farmers, miners and the Canadian Pacific railway. In return they received reservations, annual cash payments and a variety of stores and equipment, along with medical services and education for the children. The impact of disease and real deprivation that came with the destruction of the bison herds facilitated the acceptance of the treaties. They are still in place and several provinces commemorate annual treaty days.

But what is of compelling interest to Australia is that it was all done without violence. The First Nations lost much of their land. But no one was killed. The police accepted that protection of the Indigenous peoples from predatory settlers was one of their central missions. The leader of the Siksika Nation, known to the Europeans as Crowfoot, negotiated the terms of treaty number seven of 1877 and declared that the police had protected his people 'as the feathers of the bird protect it from the frosts of winter'.[3] The largely French-speaking and mixed-descent Métis took part in rebellions against the Canadian government in 1869 and 1885, but these involved few First Nations Indians and were about a different set of issues.

So why was the settlement of Western Canada so different from that of northern Australia? After all, anglophone Canada and the Australian colonies had a great deal in common, as did

120

the colonists themselves. Both were British settler colonies that had become self-governing in the middle years of the 19th century. Their political and legal systems were similar. It was very easy therefore for George Arthur to move on to Ontario after his term in Tasmania had expired, and other officials moved without difficulty between the two countries. Ontario was in a similar position to the Australian colonies in the middle of the 19th century, with British Canadian ambitions to develop the vast areas under their nominal control. The white Canadians looked west and towards the frozen north, the white Australians were endlessly concerned about their vast tropical backyard. Canadians reached towards the North Pacific, the Australians towards the Coral Sea, Torres Strait and the Arafura Sea. And the Canadian confederation of 1867 foreshadowed Australia's path to federation a generation later.

So why was the history of their late-19th-century expansion so very different? Why was one peaceful and the other particularly violent? Why did so many of Australia's First Nations people die in the process? The Canadians were aware that their story may have ended differently. They knew a great deal about America's Indian Wars and shrank from the turmoil and expense that comparable conflict would entail. America was spending more on the war with the Plains American Indians every year than the whole Canadian budget. They also wanted to differentiate themselves from their overbearing neighbour. And western Canada was unlike northern Australia. It had been the location of long and peaceful relations between Indigenous and white men, both French and British, as they worked together in the fur trade.

But perhaps even more important was the tradition of treaty-making. Treaties of one sort or another had been made by the Dutch in New York in the late 17th century, and the British adopted the same procedure. The Halifax Treaty of 1752 involved land in Nova Scotia and it was followed by many more in the Maritime Provinces (New Brunswick, Nova Scotia and Prince Edward Island). Most of the land in Ontario was subject to a series of thirty treaties negotiated between 1781 and 1862. The Robinson Treaties of 1850 concerned territory to the north of lakes Superior and Huron. So when the new Confederation bought large areas of the west from the Hudson Bay Company in 1869, it was to be expected that such well-established practices would be followed.

This leaves us with the inescapable conclusion that the British decision to abandon the policy of treaty-making in Australia had disastrous consequences for our First Nations, condemning hundreds to violent deaths. Bentham's prophecy that the failure to negotiate a treaty would be an incurable flaw runs like a dark stain through our history. Contention and fierce competition for the control of land was both inevitable and inescapable. But the British had created a situation where tensions could only be relieved by violence, as the early governors eventually discovered. And once planted in Australian soil, racial violence became habitual, expected and normalised. Both perpetrators and victims were schooled in the tradition and passed lessons learnt down the generations.

But an equally pernicious tradition grew from the failure to institute treaty-making. By their very nature treaties implied respect for the First Nations. They were peoples worthy of recognition and even grudging admiration. If not equal in all respects, and pagan rather than Christian, they were deemed to be able to understand the terms to be negotiated, could sustain an argument and had a sense of honour that made agreement-making worthwhile. Shrewd bargaining was an indication of recognisable intelligence. They were different indeed but fully human. And complex horse-trading in North America required a knowledge of Indigenous languages, forms of government and decision-making. Otherwise, how could the British be sure the appropriate interlocutors were on the other side of the table? Even more fundamental was the implication of treaty-making that the Indigenous peoples owned their hunting grounds and exercised a form of sovereignty over them. They had something valuable to bring to the table and to use in the bargaining process.

If treaty-making was a clear signal of respect, the refusal to negotiate any formal agreements at all pointed emphatically in the opposite direction. The British planned to establish their penal colony in New South Wales while viewing the First Nations with a combination of profound ignorance and cultural contempt. They were deemed to be without laws and even without permanent homelands. Above all, they were thought to require little consideration when it came to planning how the colonial project should unfold. They were not to be feared and would not stand their ground. The treaty-making tradition in North America could be safely and ethically left behind. There was no suggestion in any of the instructions given to the early governors that there was any need to consider treaties in the future. They were never mentioned.

And this quite radical departure from accustomed colonial practice was not just an oversight, an unfortunate mistake. Government and military officials would all have known something about the way the game was played in America. Many of them had only recently been involved in the War of Independence, concluded just three years before the decision was made to dispatch a large fleet to Botany Bay. The British officials turned their back on the tradition of treaty-making fully conscious of what they were doing.

George Arthur was one of the few officials who realised that a profound mistake had been made. He also came to appreciate that the old traditions were quite appropriate for Australia. His negotiation with the warriors who had been most feared left him with both regret and respect. Writing to the Colonial Office in 1833, he remarked that he found it distressing to recall the 'injuries that the Government [was] unwillingly and unavoidably made the instrument of inflicting ... of being reduced to the necessity of driving a simple but warlike, and, as it now appears, noble minded race, from their native hunting grounds'.[4] But as we have seen, he took his insights with him when he returned to Britain in 1836, and without question advised the Colonial Office of the need to return to treaty-making when it was decided to annex New Zealand.

Thirty years after Prime Minister Bob Hawke promised to negotiate a treaty at Barunga in the Northern Territory, it is state governments that have picked up the banner he left behind. The Western Australian government recently negotiated a formal agreement with the Noongar people of the south-west, which legal observers have called Australia's first treaty. Victoria, Queensland and the Northern Territory are currently at various stages along the same pathway. South Australia had begun a similar process but it was brought to a sudden end when the long-serving Labor government fell. The details of these treaties, their content and the areas to be covered are not yet known. But whatever is done at the regional level treaties will still need to be negotiated between the national government and the First Nations. Ideally, two treaties should be negotiated, one with Aboriginal Australia the other with the Torres Strait Islanders. Only then will the vexed problem of how to deal with what in the Statement from the Heart was called 'this ancient sovereignty' be resolved.

PART II

SEARCHING FOR TRUTH-TELLING

7

THE TRUTH ABOUT 26 JANUARY

Contention continues to swirl around Australia Day. It rises to a climax in January and then slowly subsides during the run-down of the year. But it never disappears and will certainly emerge again in the New Year. Marches and demonstrations held to counter public celebrations swell in size and begin to match official parades. The most striking feature of 26 January is, then, the rift in national consciousness, not collective voices of a community united in commemoration. Municipal governments in many states debate their attitude to Australia Day and increasing numbers are deciding to boycott official celebrations. Enraged conservative politicians threaten to take away their customary role in citizenship ceremonies. Their supporters in the media decry the presumed lack of loyalty both to the nation and our British heritage. Both sides dig in, and the problem of how and when to celebrate our national life and achievements becomes a focal point for the ongoing culture wars.

But for all that the contention should not evoke surprise. The problematic nature of 26 January has been apparent for a long time. It was clearly displayed in 1938 when Sydney commemorated the sesquicentenary of the arrival of the First

Fleet. While the crowds watched a replay of the British arrival, the leaders of the Aboriginal communities in Victoria and New South Wales held a Day of Mourning. Jack Patten and William Ferguson declared in a powerful pamphlet:

> The 26th of January, 1938, is not a day of rejoicing for Australia's Aborigines; it is a day of mourning. This festival of 150 years' so-called 'progress' in Australia commemorates also 150 years of misery and degradation imposed upon the original native inhabitants by the white invaders of this country ... You have almost exterminated our people, but there are enough of us remaining to expose the humbug of your claim, as white Australians, to be a civilised, progressive, kindly and humane nation.[1]

Fifty years later, Sydney was again immersed in celebration, this time for the bicentenary of the founding of white Australia. As before, the rift was inescapable. As crowds looked seaward, awaiting the arrival of a fleet of tall ships on a harbour cluttered with boats of all shapes and sizes, a huge procession, of what was calculated to be over 40 000 Aboriginal people, 'coming from all points of the southern sky', and their mainstream allies, stormed along Elizabeth Street for a rally in Hyde Park. They carried banners and wore badges that read: 'White Australia Has a Black History – Don't Celebrate 1988' and '1988 – What's to Celebrate?'. The overwhelming theme of both march and meeting was for the return of Indigenous land and reparation for two centuries of brutality and injustice. Like any good political slogan, 'White Australia Has a Black

History' used few words to encapsulate a complex freight of ideas. But concern about 26 January spreads far beyond the First Nations and their allies voicing vicarious engagement.

Opinion polls on the subject are clear about a number of things. A large majority of people want to have an occasion to commemorate our history and celebrate our way of life. This does not necessarily mean they are wedded to the present day. Nor is there evidence to suggest that those who would prefer a change of date are opposed to the idea of a distinctive national day. They are not in any meaningful sense unpatriotic, nor are they hostile to 'Australian values', the two avenues of attack by prominent defenders of the status quo. This assessment is borne out by the widespread confusion as to why 26 January was chosen in the first place. A national survey reported in *The Age* in March 2017 found that while more than seven out of ten respondents declared that Australia Day was important to them, many did not know which event it commemorated. The survey provided six alternative historical events to choose from. Only 43 per cent correctly identified the first arrival of a First Fleet ship at Sydney Cove. One in five chose the arrival of Cook on the east coast. One in six picked the anniversary of federation. Seven per cent thought the national day marked the signing of a treaty with the First Nations. Almost as many thought it was the date that commemorated the occasion when Australia ceased to be a British colony. Two per cent thought it marked an important battle during the First World War.[2]

There is a degree of perversity on display among the passionate defenders of 26 January. It made sense in the past for those who wanted to commemorate the founding of Sydney.

That was when the decision was made to move the whole expedition from Botany Bay to Sydney Harbour. It makes less sense as a day of national commemoration. There are two other dates that would be more appropriate. The first is the 20th of the month, when all the ships had arrived in Botany Bay. It was the successful conclusion of a remarkable expedition, bringing a fleet of eleven ships and over a thousand men and women from the other side of the world. It was a significant achievement of logistics and seamanship, but one of British imperial rather than Australian history. The second date is 7 February, when the formal ceremony of annexation was conducted before the whole population. The public commissions were read and, as Watkin Tench explained, the British took 'possession of the colony in form'. The marine battalion was drawn up and marched off 'with music playing and colours flying, to an adjoining ground which had been cleared for the occasion'. Once the documents had been read the officers joined Governor Arthur Phillip 'to partake of a cold collation', at which 'many loyal and public toasts were drank in commemoration of the day'.[3]

As the officers toasted the formal establishment of New South Wales, the future of relations with the local Aboriginal bands appeared propitious. The governor had good intentions and his instructions suggested he 'conciliate their affections' and enjoin 'all our subjects to live in amity and kindness with them'.[4] Tench observed that:

The Indians for a little while after our arrival paid us frequent visits, but in a few days they were observed to be

more shy of our company. From what cause their distaste
arose we could never trace, as we had made it our study,
on these occasions, to treat them with kindness, and load
them with presents. No quarrel had happened, and we had
flattered ourselves, from Governor Phillip's first reception
among them, that such a connection might be established
as would tend to the interest of both parties.[5]

Things did not turn out the way Tench expected. That had
become quite clear by the time he left the colony in December 1791. A disastrous smallpox epidemic ravaged the local
bands in April and May 1789 and then spread outward across
much of south-eastern Australia. Violence increased around
the fringes of settlement until (as mentioned in chapter 2),
in December 1790, the governor ordered Tench to lead Australia's first punitive expedition towards Botany Bay and use
terror to bring resistance to an end.

Viral epidemic was far more dramatic in its impact than
skirmishing on the edges of settlement, but it only affected
one generation. Frontier conflict became a permanent feature
of Australian life for 150 years. Disease was unpredictable.
Fighting was not. It was predetermined by the fateful decisions made in London before the First Fleet set sail. The documents read on 7 February did two things. They concerned
sovereignty and property, as we have seen above. The imperial government asserted sovereignty over the eastern half of
the continent. It was a vast and audacious claim that, as we
have already seen, would have been found illegitimate in
international law. And there were already clearly understood

protocols among the European nations about the extension of sovereignty.

What provided the British with a thin cloak of legitimacy was the assumption that no prior sovereignty existed. The First Nations had been judged from afar to have neither government nor laws and customs. And so the British officials turned their back on the tradition of treaty-making that had been alive in North America for 150 years. It is simply not possible that educated officials were unaware of already deeply entrenched policies concerning the Native Americans. The decision to regard New South Wales as a *terra nullius* was not the result of forgetfulness or inattention. The likely consequences were understood at the time. Without any means or machinery for negotiation, violence would stalk the land. It would follow the steps of frontier settlers wherever they went. Jeremy Bentham, one of the most influential thinkers of the time, recognised what was wrong with the legal foundations of the new colony. In a pamphlet that made many criticisms of official plans, he observed that there had been no negotiations with the First Nations and no treaties had been negotiated. He believed this would create enduring problems: 'The flaw is an incurable one.'[6]

An even more egregious decision was made in relation to property. In one apocalyptic moment, all the real estate over half the continent became the property of the Crown. It was an appropriation confirmed in Australian courts for 200 years. It became so central to national life that it was rarely questioned. And it cannot be distinguished from the foundation of British Australia and the commemorations of 26 January.

The mollifying thought that British behaviour was quite normal, even acceptable, in the late 18th century provides little in the way of defence. No justification can be found in the international law of the period or in currently accepted behaviour of nation states. The scale of the expropriation was without precedent, and once again only made sense if it was accepted that the First Nations had never been in actual possession of their homelands and that over vast stretches of land there were no settled inhabitants and that there was neither land law nor tenure.

Everything changed in 1992 when the High Court handed down its judgment in the *Mabo* case. The judges overthrew 200 years of legal precedent, deciding that before the arrival of the British invaders the First Nations had both settled inhabitants and land law. They were the legitimate owners of their ancestral homelands. As Justice Brennan declared in the imperishable words, the Meriam people were 'entitled against the whole world to possession, occupation, use and enjoyment' of their traditional land.[7]

The implication was inescapable. The British had expropriated the land without compensation. It was a land grab almost without precedent. And by its very nature revolutionary in the same way as was the Bolshevik's abolition of private property in 1917. How this expropriation could have happened under the aegis of the common law is hard to explain. Because at the same moment and by the same legal instruments the land was expropriated, the Aboriginal peoples all over New South Wales became British subjects, so-called beneficiaries of the King's peace. Australian judges have often dated the assumption of ownership from either 1786 when Phillip received his first commission or from the formal annexation on 7 February 1788. Is that when the incorporation occurred? Both at the same time? Or did one precede the other? These seemingly arcane questions matter because they bring us to the much broader question of the sanctity bestowed on private property by the common law.

The right to private property was central both to British political philosophy and law. The pivotal thinker John Locke argued that there were three natural rights – to life, liberty and property. He defined power as the 'right of making laws, with penalties of death, and consequently all less penalties, for the regulating and preserving of property'. He believed that men entered society in the first place in order to protect their possessions, explaining that 'the great and chief end of men entering into commonwealths' was 'the preservation of their property'. What is more, no government could 'take from any man any part of his property without his consent'. The state could legitimately take a man's life but it could not confiscate his estate. The proposition that anyone could actually lose their property as a result of entering society was 'too gross an absurdity for any man to own'.[8] The relevance of these sentiments for the Aboriginal peoples needs little accentuation.

One of the central themes in the history of the common law was the centuries-long struggle to defend the property of the subject from appropriation by the Crown. Statutes of the 13th and 14th centuries were designed to restrain the arbitrary power of kings to confiscate the property of their subjects. And the fight against prerogative power persisted. The common law had for centuries built up powerful barriers around the property of the subject. Indeed, it was 'not more solicitous of anything than "to preserve the property of the subject from the inundation of the prerogative"'.[9] The 17th-century jurist Sir Christopher Yelverton explained 'that no man's property can be legally taken from him or invaded by the direct act or command of the sovereign, without the consent of the subject ... is *jus indigenae*, an old home-born right, declared to be law by divers statutes of the realm'.[10]

It is important to remember that New South Wales was regarded as a colony of settlement. British law arrived with the First Fleet. Early legal and administrative decisions made it clear that the prerogative power of the Crown was no more extensive in Sydney than in Britain itself.[11] So how had the Crown acquired the landed property of First Nations across vast stretches of territory without their permission and without providing compensation? It had been stolen from people who were subjects within the King's peace. And how and why was this outstanding anomaly allowed to determine what happened to tens of thousands of men, women and children for 200 years? So much of the violence on the frontier was occasioned by settlers enforcing the expropriation of tribal land that had the sanction of the law. Colonial life was brutal at times, but the moral responsibility belongs to the British officials who determined the conditions resulting from the plans they developed for the annexation of the country. And ultimately, it was the responsibility of the British Crown, which made no attempt to protect the First Nations from the inundation of the prerogative. And so the 'tide of settlement' advanced 'along an ever widening line, breaking the tribes with its first waves and overwhelming their wrecks with its flood'.[12]

Another astonishing anomaly that the proponents of 26 January as our national day often assert is that the First Fleet brought with it the rule of law. It is less than obvious how such a claim can be sustained. In 1788 the law was profoundly subverted. Hundreds of years of tradition were overturned. For anyone to lose their property as a result of being incorporated into British society was, as Locke had insisted, too gross an absurdity for any man to own. Do the flag-wavers have any idea what they are urging us to commemorate? Do they not know? Do they care?

And then there is the question of hypocrisy. Many nations find it difficult to avoid when they commemorate their past. One of the best known examples is the United States and the Declaration of Independence, with its famous assertion that all men are born equal and endowed with inalienable rights to life, liberty and the pursuit of happiness. Of the fifty-six men who signed the document forty-six either were, or had been, slave owners. George Washington owned 300, Jefferson a mere 100. Australians have given little thought to their own comparable problem. But if Australia had a founding principle, it was the sanctity of private property. The imperial government had a number of motives when it decided to plant a settlement on the east coast of Australia, but punishment for crimes against property was central to the whole operation. The convicts were wrenched from homeland, community and family, in most cases for theft. Their punishment was designed as a deterrent against future transgression. The story is well known. And the full force of laws against theft was imposed from the moment the expedition arrived in Sydney. At the end of February 1788, five men were convicted of theft and condemned to death, illustrating that property was more sacrosanct than life itself. The sentences were carried out at public hangings, which the whole convict population was forced to watch. Just three weeks before, half a continent had been declared Crown land in one of the most remarkable acts of plunder in modern times. It may well be argued that the British thought the land belonged to no one. But that was not an explanation that was taken very seriously if convicts tried the same excuse when they came face to face with the magistrates.

There are so many reasons not to commemorate the nation on 26 January. Aboriginal and Torres Strait Islander people have made their feelings plain since at least 1938 and continue to do so. It is surely extraordinary that their opposition has been disregarded. And it is not as if they didn't have a strong case. The arrival in January 1788 did not merely presage disasters that were to follow. It was the precise moment when the tragedy began relentlessly to unfold. And once the British claimed both the sovereignty and all the property, there was no turning back. The dark seeds of disaster had been sown. Like people everywhere who have suffered from deep, collective tragedies, it is pointless and gratuitous to tell Indigenous Australians to get over it and to look to the future. John Locke understood the pain felt by the dispossessed and their right to struggle for reparation. He thought that the inhabitants of any country, who are descended, and derive a title to their estates from those who are subdued, and had a government forced upon them against their free consents, retain a right to the possessions of their ancestors … [they] have always a right to … free themselves from the usurpation or tyranny which the sword hath brought in upon them.

The struggle to regain land unjustly taken might well proceed generation upon generation. 'If it be objected', Locke declared, 'this would cause endless trouble; I answer, no more than justice does, where she lies open to all that appeal to her.'[13]

An argument frequently heard in the testy debate about Australia Day is that what happened to the Aboriginal peoples resulted from what was regarded as acceptable behaviour at the time. That is just what happened in the 18th century, the argument runs, and it is pointless now to make judgments using the ideas and sensibility of contemporary times. It is anachronistic at best and 'virtue signalling' at worst. But as previous discussions have illustrated, British behaviour in Australia in the late 18th and early 19th centuries had little support from the writing of international jurists, nor did it follow well-trodden paths of precedent long laid down in North America. And while modern human rights discourse emerged well after 1788, the right to property was, by then, deeply embedded in British law and politics.

But the judgments we make today can't eschew contemporary ideas and sensibility. On any measure, the First Nations suffered grievously as a result of the British annexation. They were the victims of profound injustice. The early ethnographers Fison and Howitt saw it as it was. 'The advance of settlement', they wrote in 1880, 'upon the frontier at least' was 'marked by a line of blood'.[14] Peace of a kind arrived everywhere sooner or later, but the suffering persisted. Demographic recovery took over a century in many places. Death frequently came early for survivors of the wars, and few children were born or survived their early years. Poverty and despair were found everywhere.

Even now, many Australians find it hard to accept that white Australia does, indeed, have a black history. Their desire to commemorate 26 January arises from the felt need to focus on both our British heritage and the ongoing story of successful nation-building. John Howard was fond of saying that our history had a few blemishes. Scott Morrison remarked recently that colonisation did produce 'a few scars from some mistakes and things that [we] could have done better'.[15] These comments may have been made in passing, but they are symptomatic of problems that are much more than skin deep.

How are we to explain this singular failure of empathy? Why is the profound injustice visited upon the First Nations not treated with the appropriate gravity? Why continue to commemorate a day that takes the nation back to where it all began? And, for that matter, why identify so completely with the imperial invaders? Why have Australian leaders never asked for an apology from the British government or from the Queen herself in the manner pursued by the Māori? And why not suggest that some form of reparation would be appropriate for a land seizure completely at odds with the common law? The apostles of our current Australia Day expect

Aboriginal and Torres Strait Islander people to be loyal members of the Australian state and would react strongly against any hint of separatism. But do they really think they are part of the nation? Are they white Australians' countrymen and -women? If so, why can't all Australians identify with them and feel their pain?

8

SETTLEMENT, CONQUEST OR SOMETHING ELSE?

The British messed up the colonisation of Australia. We still live with the consequences 230 years later. They departed from the practice, well established in North America, of signing treaties with the Indigenous nations and recognising their land rights. Instead they claimed to have acquired Australia by a process of peaceful settlement. That assertion remains at the heart of Australian law to this day. There is comfort in the idea. 'Settlement' after all has a soothing sound to it. And its many meanings convey suggestions of coming to rest, of fixing securely, of establishing tranquillity, of quietening or composing. They are clearly meanings far removed from the gritty, turbulent and often bloody business of colonisation.

But there are much more substantial objections to the whole concept of untroubled acquisition. It was premised on the conviction that the First Nations were without law; were wandering hordes without established homelands. They were naked savages whose manner of life placed them far below Europeans on the great chain of being. We have not been able to escape from this source of ideas that still flow through our jurisprudence, even if they come from European attitudes that were in vogue 200 years ago. In 1979 Justice Lionel Murphy described the idea of peaceful settlement as a 'convenient falsehood'.[1] Convenience is no longer a good enough reason to preserve a concept that is totally out of place in modern Australia.

Discussion in this book has already outlined the way colonial reality quickly undermined the intellectual and moral foundations of *terra nullius*. Within a few years it was obvious that the Aboriginal nations lived in clearly defined territories that they defended against all intruders, whether Aboriginal or European. They had distinct languages and traditions, which suggested the territorial boundaries were of ancient origin. Within a generation, observers in New South Wales and Tasmania had come to appreciate that the distinct nations had their own forms of law and government. So the gap progressively widened between the way the law was understood and experience gathered around the frontiers of settlement, which was disseminated in books and newspaper articles, speeches and sermons. Policy and opinion developed what could be called conceptual dissonance. There was, as a result, sharp disagreement about the whole basis of the colonisation. Public debate showed up the confusion about the morality, the legality and even the decency of the way the project was unfolding.

It was Aboriginal resistance that presented the greatest challenge, and it erupted whenever settlers pushed out into new territory. Repression in one district had little impact elsewhere. Immigrants from the urban areas of England and

Scotland found themselves in unexpected situations. Many of them would never have used a gun. And it was hard to escape the regular reports of violent conflict in the newspapers published in Sydney, Hobart and Launceston. It upset so many assumptions. The more idealistic colonists thought the poor savages would be uplifted by their example and the collective tutelage of the white men. They would acquire attributes of civilisation and through conversion aspire to salvation. But that's not the way it turned out. The Aboriginal peoples were recalcitrant. Their own beliefs prevailed, manifesting an unexpected resilience. Converts to British ways or to Christianity were hard to find.

By the 1820s, the impact of colonisation was clear in the closely settled districts of New South Wales and Tasmania. The local Aboriginal bands were massively outnumbered and new shiploads of convicts and free settlers were arriving every few weeks. The Aboriginal groups lived in poverty on the fringes of the towns, and their numbers continued to decline as a result of premature death and dwindling birth rates. The comforting notions of peaceful settlement and a benign British presence were hard to sustain. Responses varied. A correspondent wrote to the *Port Phillip Gazette* in 1842, observing that, 'the irretrievable step of taking possession of a country, infers many minor wrongs to its inhabitants, besides the first great act of spoliation; but he who would govern in a country so situated, must steel his breast to their wrongs which are unanswerable ...'[2] Not everyone could so fortify their conscience. In a long letter written to a British missionary society in 1826, a 'Gentleman in New South Wales' declared:

Yes Sir, strange to say, Civilization has been a scourge
to the Natives; Disease, Crime, Misery and Death have
hitherto been the sure attendants of our intercourse with
them. Wherever we trace the steps of white population
we discover the introduction of evil, the diminution of
numbers, the marks of disease, the pressure of want, the
physical and moral ruin of this people ... Could we but
trace each poor individual's history what a tale it would
unfold! Sir, it is a sad truth that *our prosperity has hitherto
been their ruin, our increase their destruction. The history of
nearly forty years seals the veracity of this declaration.*

With such recollections as these fresh in our minds
with what pleasure can we possibly survey the rapid
encroachment of the whites on these unhappy people.
With what feelings can we look forward, but with those
of deep regret, when we are assured that every new step
which advances our interests is fatal to their existence.
That every acre of land reclaimed by our industry is so
much wrested from that pittance which Providence has
bestowed on them.

... what will future generations think of our boasted
Christianity, of our lauded Philanthropy, when our
posterity read in the early page of Australian history the
misery and ruin which marked our adoption of this land;–
when they find recorded that our proprietorship of the
soil has been purchased at such a costly sacrifice of human
happiness and life.[3]

But if the British did not acquire Australia by peaceful occupation, how did it happen? It was a subject of frequent public debate. GA Robinson expressed his doubts about the matter in a letter to a friend in 1832. He explained that he was at a loss 'to conceive by what tenure we hold this country for it does not appear to be that we either hold it by right of conquest or right of purchase'.[4] After touring Australia, Colonel GC Mundy had similar doubts: 'We hold it neither by inheritance, by purchase, nor by conquest, but by a sort of gradual eviction. As our flocks and herds and population increase, and space is required, the natural owners of the soil are thrust back without treaty, bargain or apology.'[5] While it was clear to everyone that no treaties had been negotiated, the question of conquest was another matter altogether. And it was often discussed in the colonial newspapers. The violence that accompanied colonisation pointed to conquest rather than peaceful occupation, and allowed for comforting comparison with violent acquisition by other nations in various times and places.

'It is evident that New Holland is only held by right of might', a New South Wales colonist argued in 1843.[6] A few years later a correspondent writing to a Brisbane paper agreed, observing that 'We have seized their country by the right of might, and by the right of might the whites will continue to possess it.'[7] A contemporary wrote to the same paper a little later declaring: 'We hold this country by the right of conquest and … that right gives us a just claim to its continual possession.'[8] The prominent Western Australian lawyer Edward Landor wrote the most powerful polemic in favour of conquest in his book *The Bushman, or Life in a New Country*, published in 1847. It is so cogent it merits quoting at length:

> Nothing could be more anomalous and perplexing than the position of the Aborigines as British subjects. Our brave and conscientious Britons, whilst taking possession of their territory, have been most careful and anxious to make it universally known, that Australia is not a conquered country; and successive Secretaries of State … have repeatedly commanded that it must never be forgotten 'that our possession of this territory *is based on a right of occupancy.*'
>
> A 'right of occupancy!' Amiable sophistry! Why not say boldly at once, the right of power? We have seized upon the country, and shot down the inhabitants, until the survivors have found it expedient to submit to our rule … On what grounds can we possibly claim a *right* to the occupancy of the land? …
>
> We have a right to our Australian possessions; but it is the right of Conquest, and we hold them with the grasp of Power. Unless we proceed on this foundation, our conduct towards the native population can be considered only as a monstrous absurdity. However Secretaries of State may choose to phrase the matter, we can have no other *right* of occupancy. We resolve to found a colony in a country, the inhabitants of which are not strong enough to prevent our so doing, though they evince their repugnance by a thousand acts of hostility.[9]

Like many colonists, Landor was perplexed about the problem of applying British law to the Aboriginal peoples. 'What right', he asked, 'have we to impose laws upon a people whom we profess not to have conquered' and have never 'annexed themselves or their country to the British Empire by any written or even verbal treaty?'

So is conquest the best answer to the question 'How did Britain gain possession of Australia?' Contemporary debate suggests that the idea has devotees. It has a no-nonsense simplicity and is certainly as plausible as the 'convenient falsehood' of peaceful occupation. And conquest was a legally permissible way to acquire sovereignty until after the Second World War. But conceptual problems abound. The overarching one is not just how the acquisition was effected but when. And this is a problem for both contending interpretations. The claim that in either 1786 or 1788 Britain gained sovereignty over the whole of eastern Australia falls at the first interrogation and was not taken seriously in the Colonial Office as early as the 1830s. How could the Empire assume authority over people and places that had never been seen and in many cases would be beyond contact for generations to come? It must be understood not as a 'convenient falsehood' but rather as a convenient fantasy. It suggests that Britain gained a continent at the stroke of a pen. Would there ever have been a more graphic illustration of the old saying that the pen is mightier than the sword?

But the converts to conquest also face difficulties. As we have seen above, conquest concerned sovereignty not property. Citizens of a defeated nation acquired a new sovereign. He or she did not acquire their property. And if First Nations' sovereignty did not disappear in one apocalyptic moment, it must have happened gradually and incrementally. But how? If we take the idea of conquest seriously, we must consider whose sovereignty was at stake. It would be totally inappropriate to refer to 'the Aborigines' or to 'Indigenous Australia'. We have to deal with the small nations that actually exercised sovereignty over their ancestral territories. Each one would have to be considered separately. There is no other way to deal with the question. Detailed historical investigation could detail when the invaders arrived, how fighting began, how long it lasted and when it ended. But even that would not resolve the big question. Did the intrusion of small, albeit aggressive, parties of white men and vast numbers of domestic animals represent an assertion of sovereignty? And when, specifically, did the new sovereign hold the territory in what Landor termed 'the grasp of Power'? Without a peace treaty, when was the matter finalised? And did the First Nations actually concede that they had been defeated? In most cases they continued to live on their land and to impose their own laws and customs even if in many cases it involved a diminished band of survivors. Did locals and newcomers share a form of dual sovereignty?

The problems that perplexed our ancestors did not melt away. In fact, they were serious enough to be considered by the Senate Standing Committee on Constitutional and Legal Affairs in 1983. The problem the members addressed resulted from Australia's situation where, they concluded, 'no clear title to sovereignty can be shown by way of occupation, conquest or cession'. This seemed to be the case even though the territory in question had remained under continuous and undisputed sovereignty for so long that the position had become part of the established international order of nations. To remedy the situation they turned to what they called the 'rule of prescription', which they believed would necessarily apply to overturn the defect and securely vest sovereign title in the Commonwealth of Australia.[10] It sounded very reassuring. But the committee's confidence was not securely based for a number of reasons. There was no attempt to distinguish between external and internal sovereignty. This was perhaps not surprising. The difference between the two is infrequently discussed and little understood. External sovereignty concerns the relationship between nation states. Internal sovereignty refers to the exercise of power, law and authority within the nation state. When it comes to external sovereignty, the British claim has been undisputed for a long time. But it is impossible to sustain that assertion in relation to internal sovereignty. That is what a century and more of frontier conflict was all about. That is why First Nations leaders have recently claimed at least remnant sovereignty in the Uluru Statement.

And then there is the matter of prescription, which needs some explaining. The concept of prescription or adverse possession has been entrenched in British law for a very long time. The basic premise is that long use of another's property eventually creates rights based on unchallenged use. In domestic law, occupation, undisturbed and peaceful, of twenty years' standing is sufficient to convert occupation into ownership. Its relevance to the matter in hand will be obvious. And the same principles have been incorporated into international law. But occupation by one party only tells us half the story. There also has to be acquiescence on the part of the original owner. In his 1965 study, *Historic Titles in International Law*, Yehuda Blum explained that from the legal point of view it was 'not the fact of effective possession, but rather the presumption of acquiescence, that sets the seal of legal validity on the historic claim'.[11] This principle had been secure in international law for a long time. In his 1854 *Commentaries upon International Law*, British judge Robert Phillimore observed that prescription must be 'founded upon a presumption of voluntary abandonment' by former owners. A forcible and unjust seizure of country, 'which the inhabitants, overpowered for the moment by the superiority of physical force, ineffectually resist', is a possession that would lack 'an originally just title'.[12]

It would be very hard indeed to establish that the Aboriginal peoples acquiesced in the loss of their own country. They didn't abandon their places as Joseph Banks predicted. They resisted the invasion. David Collins, later lieutenant governor of Van Diemen's Land, observed that around the first settlement the local bands regarded the British as enemies, whom they made a point of attacking whenever opportunity and safety concurred. It is doubtful if any of the many small nations thought they had lost their claim to the land of their ancestors. Without treaties there could be no formal concession. And even in those places where they had been outnumbered by the interlopers, they evinced 'their repugnance by a thousand acts of hostility', in the words of Landor.

The members of the Senate Committee on Constitutional and Legal Affairs turned to international law to resolve the question of how Britain acquired Australia, and the same is true of judges who have been asked to construe the question of sovereignty. But there is more to this desire to look at Australia from the outside than many observers imagine. Colonial and even early federation Australias have to be seen as being players in the great contemporary drama arising from the late upsurge of European imperialism. Australia's moving frontier was one manifestation of British imperialism and should be considered according to the international law and the practice of nations at the time. And that differed from the way things were considered locally, where the standard view was that all questions relating to sovereignty and the legal status of the First Nations had been put beyond question as far back as 1788.

Before federation, the first Australian prime minister declared that federation would create 'a nation for a continent and a continent for a nation'.[13] It was a happy conceit but it was not what outsiders would have seen if they had looked at the continent from beyond our borders. Australia in 1901 was far from being a normal nation state. Geography and history had seen to that. It was still a British colony with very limited external sovereignty. It had no independent international standing. When it came to internal sovereignty, the picture was even more complicated. And yet Melbourne, as the initial seat of federal government, was an imperial capital with its own empire, albeit all contained within the confines of the continent. There were three quite distinct regions. To begin with there were the areas of early and heaviest colonisation. These included the cities and towns and the farming and mining districts. This was where the bulk of the incoming population lived, but by 1901 many of them were Australian-born. The Aboriginal population had long been swamped. By the early 20th century, people of mixed descent were about to become a majority in many regions. In this archipelago of settled districts, government exercised full administrative control and effectively enforced the introduced legal code. It probably covered less than half the continent, although exact measurement would be very difficult.

The second region covered the vast rangelands, which small parties of Europeans had occupied from the 1830s with their flocks and herds. Some districts were taken over by farmers, but that barely changed the overall situation. In 1901 the pastoral industry occupied up to a third of the continent. The European population was very small, overwhelmingly male and incessantly itinerant. In many places there were more Aboriginal people than white men, and they provided much of the labour for the stations. There was little administrative control and the imposition of the law was at best rudimentary.

The third region began where the pastoral invasion had stalled, brought to a halt by the vast arid interior, rugged hill country and coastal wetlands. There was a lot of it – the central deserts, significant parts of Cape York, all of Arnhem Land, the offshore islands and the more inaccessible parts of the Kimberley. Here there was almost no permanent European presence. Many districts were unexplored by Europeans and unmapped. Aboriginal life was virtually untouched.

Traditional ways persisted. Law and custom prevailed. And all along the north coast the Saltwater people hosted the Indonesian fishermen who had been spending the months of the wet season on the coast for generations.

Situations like this were common in the late 19th century, although they were more to be expected in colonies separated from the imperial capital by the oceans of the world and not like Australia, where Melbourne was separated by vast stretches of little visited land. But the basic principles were the same. A study of international law at the time allows us to categorise the Australian situation. Over the second, pastoral region the new federal government exercised less than plenary powers. What it could legitimately claim was not full sovereignty but what was known at the time as a protectorate. These were regions where the British Crown had acquired 'a portion of the territorial sovereignty of a state or tribal community' short of complete annexation. The exclusion of foreign states was the primary object, consequently external sovereignty was appropriated but only 'so much of the internal sovereignty' as was 'needed to be its complement'.[14] In the third, uninvaded region control was even more tenuous than it was in a protectorate, and would have been considered at the time as a sphere of influence, which was defined as: 'the regions which geographically are adjacent to or politically group themselves naturally with, possessions or protectorates, but which have not actually been so reduced into control that the minimum of the powers which are implied in a protectorate can be exercised with tolerable regularity'.[15]

Australian jurists have avoided dealing with the problems arising from the way the British claimed sovereignty over

Australia. They have suggested on numerous occasions that a full understanding of the matters involved required a consideration of international law. But it does not seem that there are any easy answers there. And so the same questions still remain there, towering over us all.

9

THE COST OF CONQUEST

Many people died during the conquest of Australia's First Nations, men, women and children. And the killing went on for a long time. It accompanied the growth and expansion of Australia for 140 years. It is, quite simply, one of the most important chapters of our national story. It is unavoidable. But it has always been a matter of controversy. Many opinions have clashed from as far back as the early 19th century. Collectively, they add urgent voices to our 200-year-old political and moral discourse. But the contention has largely been contained within settler society. It was the central theme of my book *This Whispering in Our Hearts*.[1] There is little disagreement in the Indigenous community about the overwhelming importance of what has become known as the 'killing times'. Catastrophes of the kind experienced by so many people can never be easily or entirely forgotten. Forgiveness is always possible but it cannot alter the irreducible facts about what happened. That is why history has remained at the centre of the ideological cockpit. Contention is inevitably untethered when the past is commemorated and achievements celebrated. This is reflected in the annual disputes about Australia Day and the debate about the significance of the 250th anniversary of Cook's voyage along the east coast. It was particularly apparent in 1988, when white Australia chose to party with exuberant emptiness in tune with the song: 'Celebration of the Nation: Let's make it great in '88'. But we can see now, thirty years later, that the most enduring monument to the bicentenary was *The Aboriginal Memorial*, an installation of Yolngu burial poles now in pride of place in the National Gallery in Canberra.

It came from the Yolngu community Ramingining in Arnhem Land and was an adaptation of traditional burial poles of the clans whose home country straddled the Clyde River. The original idea came from the Bandjalung curator, activist and artist Djon Mundine, who was working in the community at the time. He was alerted by John Pilger's documentary *The Secret Country* to the fact that while Australia had hundreds of war memorials to soldiers who had fought and fallen overseas, there was nothing comparable to commemorate the people of the First Nations who had died defending their homelands. And so the idea was born to paint 200 burial poles, one for each year of British settlement. The project attracted the participation of forty-three men and women. Mundine explained that the installation would be 'like a forest – a forest like a large war cemetery, a war memorial for all those Aboriginal people who died defending their country'.[2] The installation remains a greatly admired artwork, revered by the National Gallery and attracting large crowds when displayed overseas. But it also remains a controversial installation for settler Australians and that, after all, was the point of all the collective industry. Frontier violence is still a contested topic and has been since the early 19th century. And Mundine's central challenge about the absence of memorials for the frontier wars is as relevant today as it was in 1988.

For pioneers out on the fringes of settlement, conflict was an everyday reality. They were often outnumbered by the bands whose land they had occupied. They feared sudden attack and a spear in the back. Enough white men were injured and killed to continually fortify their fear. And in some places they suffered from acute anxiety for years on end. They carried guns wherever they went and kept them within reach when they were camping and sleeping. They believed they were engaged in a life-and-death struggle. Personal enrichment merged in their minds with the advance of 'civilisation' or the expansion of the Empire. They were strengthened by the support and understanding of the frontier community. They rallied when parties gathered to search for the elusive warriors and attacked them when they came across a camp. They had the camaraderie of conspirators. What happened out in the bush became encircled in secrecy and the details were never reported anywhere. Even if they were alluded to in the small frontier newspapers, they were carefully phrased using well-known, generally understood euphemisms. But distance was the greatest ally of the assassins. Once the settlers had crossed the Blue Mountains in the early 1820s, the resulting conflict moved further and further into the vast interior, beyond the scrutiny of the government and away from the consciousness of the increasingly urban population. Immigrants left their ships in the port cities and many stayed there, and the same was true of children born in the towns. By the middle of the

19th century, fewer and fewer colonists had ever had personal experience of frontier warfare.

But controversy about violent conflict was ever present. There were always humanitarian colonists who took up the cause of the Aboriginal peoples and who wrote letters to newspapers in the cities and in Britain. Many pulpits rang with denunciation of bloodshed, and like-minded campaigners petitioned governments to bring some order to the lawless frontiers. No educated colonist could have been unaware of the violence that accompanied the expansion of both frontier mining and the pastoral industry. In Queensland in 1880, the whole reading public was confronted by a months-long crusade by the leading weekly paper *The Queenslander* denouncing the whole process of violent dispossession. In editorials and in the large number of letters from readers, the colony debated the nature and the morality of the whole colonial project. But here, as elsewhere at the time, there was no doubt about the attendant violence and the indiscriminate killing. What was at stake was the question of whether violence was necessary or not. Reports of mass killing passed without contention. They were clearly widely known. No one suggested that reports of frontier violence were exaggerated or made up. What the controversialists debated was whether violence was a necessary instrument of successful colonisation, a precondition of their own secure and comfortable lives.

While Queensland was locked in fierce debate about the colony's short, brutal history, the Victorian pioneer Edward Curr was compiling much of the then available knowledge about the Aboriginal peoples. To learn all he could about the

recent history of European expansion, he corresponded with
settlers all over Australia. His findings, published in 1886,
were important, representing what was generally known at
the time. He had no doubt about the violence of the frontier,
writing:

> In the first place the meeting of the Aboriginal tribes of
> Australia and the White pioneer, results as a rule in war,
> which lasts from six months to ten years, according to the
> nature of the country, the amount of settlement which
> takes place in a neighbourhood, and the proclivities of the
> individuals concerned. When several squatters settle in
> proximity, and the country they occupy is easy of access
> and without fastnesses to which the Blacks can retreat,
> the period of warfare is usually short and the bloodshed
> not excessive. On the other hand, in districts which are
> not easily traversed on horseback, in which the Whites
> are few in number and food is procurable by the Blacks in
> fastnesses, the term is usually prolonged and the slaughter
> more considerable.

Curr concluded that the 'slaughter' resulted in a high death
toll. He estimated that from 15 to 25 per cent of the original
population fell 'by the rifle'.[3]

It is quite clear then that by the 1880s, well-informed
Australians knew a lot about frontier conflict. This should
not come as a surprise. It had been an ever present characteristic of European expansion for almost a hundred years.
And it was still raging right across the tropical north. What is

more intriguing is that it was openly talked about in the newspapers, in the colonial parliaments, in books and articles, and presumably in private conversations. There was no debate about whether the killing had taken place and was still happening. That was a given. Few people argued that such frank discussion was out of place, imprudent or even unpatriotic. The men, like Edward Curr, who led the debate were able to look back to the early years of colonisation. They often knew from personal experience what it was like to live on, or close to, the frontier. But there was no squeamish avoidance of the history of violence and brutality. They knew and accepted that killing was an intrinsic part of colonisation. The themes that ran through much of the public discussion were whether the killing had been necessary or more extensive than required. Could it have been avoided? How could things change? And perhaps even more portentously, what future was there for the First Nations as the ever expanding colonies already looked forward to federation and beckoning national greatness?

But whatever happened? Why, eighty years later, did one of the country's most distinguished anthropologists, WEH Stanner, feel it necessary to call out the country's historians for having discarded all that knowledge and understanding of the colonial past? Indeed, the Aboriginal peoples had been consciously excluded from the national story. His contemporaries were guilty of perpetuating what he called the 'great Australian silence'. Inattention on such a scale could 'not be explained by absent-mindedness'. Rather it was a 'structural matter'. They had habitually taken in 'a view from a window which has been carefully placed to exclude a whole quadrant of the landscape'. What may have begun 'as a simple forgetting of other possible views turned under habit and over time into something like a cult of forgetfulness practised on a national scale'.[4]

The great forgetting is one of the most important aspects of Australian intellectual and cultural life during the first sixty years of the 20th century. How on earth did it happen? And why? This was the time when the ANZAC legend was evolving and the phrase 'Lest We Forget' acquired iconic status. It meant that two and even three generations of Australians were nurtured with a national story that left out much of the most significant aspects of their colonial heritage. Why did they become less able to deal with the reality of the killing times than their fathers and grandfathers who had been there and who had acquired a reputation for exaggerated reticence?

One of the contributing influences was the overwhelming belief that the Aboriginal people were a dying race with no long-term future. Shrinking populations in many parts of the country pointed in this direction. But arching over observed demographic developments was the all-pervasive influence of Social Darwinism, which provided what was thought to be the scientific evidence for the inevitable decline and eventual passing of the race. These ideas had both intellectual respectability and broad popular acceptance. But, in itself, that does not explain the disappearance of the First Nations from the history books that was underway in the early years of federation and was not reversed until the last decades of the 20th century. With very few exceptions, histories of Australia began either with the arrival of the First Fleet or the voyages of the European navigators. Many books referred to the Aboriginal presence in early New South Wales and considered the conflict in Tasmania in the 1820s. But that was usually where scholarly attention dropped away and in most cases did not resume again. Readers would have assumed that apart from those early years, the Aboriginal peoples played no significant part in the national story. In 1938, Stanner observed that the 'disappearance of the tribes' was 'not commonly regarded as a present and continuing tragedy, but (for some curious reason) rather as something which took place a long time ago, in the very early days, and so is no longer a real complication'.[5]

It does not appear that anyone much minded or thought there was something missing in the way national history was interpreted. In a book for children written in 1917, Walter Murdoch, one of the country's most distinguished literary scholars, explained that when people talked about the history of Australia,

> they mean the history of the white people who have lived
> in Australia. There is a good reason why we should not
> stretch the term to make it include the story of the dark-
> skinned wandering tribes who hurled boomerangs and ate
> snakes in their native land for long ages before the arrival
> of the first intruders from Europe ... He [the historian]
> is concerned with Australia only as the dwelling-place
> of white men and women, settlers from overseas. It is his
> business to tell us how these white folk found the land,
> how they settled in it, how they explored it and how they
> gradually made it the Australia we know to-day.[6]

WK Hancock wrote the most important history of Australia in the first half of the 20th century. He devoted one paragraph to the Aboriginal peoples, whose response to the European invasion was, he insisted, 'pathetically helpless'. He thought it might be possible to save a remnant of the race on controlled reserves, but it would 'cost hard thought and hard cash'. From time to time, he observed, Australia 'remembers the primitive people whom it has dispossessed, and sheds over their predestined passing an economical tear'.[7] The profession made little progress in the next thirty years. In 1959, Professor John La Nauze from the Australian National University addressed a meeting of his colleagues and surveyed the historical work that had been written during the three decades since the publication of Hancock's book. He observed that lack of interest in the Aboriginal peoples was one of the striking characteristics of national historiography. He thought this was because Australia was unique among settler societies in having 'no real experience of formidable opposition from the native inhabitants'. Unlike the Māori, the American Indians or the Bantu, the Indigenous Australians were noticed in our history 'only in a melancholy anthropological footnote'.[8] It was a common view at the time. In his 1966 book *Empire in the Antipodes: The British in Australasia 1840–1860*, JM Ward scarcely noticed the Aboriginal peoples, and when he did it was to make invidious comparison with the Māori who, he assured his readers, were a proud warlike people who 'could not be relegated to obscurity in the same way as the aboriginals of Australia'.[9] A year earlier, Russel Ward published a general history of Australia in which he asserted that the nation had a uniquely peaceful history because of the 'mild Aborigines', whose reaction to settler intrusion was 'so sporadic and ineffectual that men seldom had to go armed on the Australian frontier'.[10] This was a most surprising assessment. But above all it was wrong. Frontier districts bristled with guns. This had been true for a hundred years. And Ward's signature work was his study of the nomad tribe of bush workers published as *The Australian Legend* in 1958. There was nothing in the book about the often violent relations between the First Nations and the pastoral workforce.

So how did Australia forget the truth about the killing times and the violent frontier? It had once been common knowledge. Part of the answer is that with the Aboriginal peoples relegated to an 'anthropological footnote,' almost all the domestic violence dropped out of sight with them. And even when discussed, it was with reference to the early years of settlement, suggesting that it had all happened a long time ago. There was a deep attachment to the story of a society whose history was uniquely peaceful. This was a theme that ran through Douglas Pike's general history of 1962, entitled *Australia: The Quiet Continent*.[11] Leading historians took pride in their belief that Australians have been 'remarkably slow to kill each other'.[12] But there was also a conscious endeavour to hide the shocking truth about the long history of bloodshed. In numerous books there are references to the need to 'draw a veil over the sad picture' or to draw the curtain over it all.[13] The celebrated ethnographers Baldwin Spencer and FJ Gillen wrote that there were parts of Australia 'where it is well to draw a veil over the past history of the relationship between the blackfellow and the white man'.[14]

This tradition ran on into the post-war period. In writing his *Black Australians*, Paul Hasluck exercised a form of self-imposed censorship. It was not possible to completely ignore the violence on the Western Australian frontier, but he explained that in the 'scant references to violence, no more will be quoted than seems necessary to show the measures taken or the attitude of the colonists'.[15] In her 1963 *History of Australia*, Marjorie Barnard thought that little was to be gained 'by recounting all the recorded black and white incidents'.[16] At much the same time, the distinguished medical scientist JB Cleland thought it was a 'matter of deep regret that atrocities committed by unscrupulous white people on our natives years ago are raked up and recounted ... for propaganda purposes'.[17] And that was the state of play when in 1966 I began teaching Australian history in a new, small university college in North Queensland.

I was poorly prepared for the task in front of me. Very little Australian history had been offered at the University of Tasmania where I did my Arts degree. I knew almost nothing about Aboriginal history or the legacy of the frontier wars. What I did know would have conformed to the general ideas current at the time. But North Queensland provided graphic, totally unexpected lessons about the whole complex of relations between white Australia and the Aboriginal and Torres Strait Islander peoples who made up a substantial minority of the population. And the history of frontier violence was much closer there than in the south and still shadowed the present. The importance of race was confirmed out there in the public almost every day. My students had grown up encircled by tense ambience.

After my first year's teaching I decided I must start incorporating these themes into my lectures. But how? The course content was determined by the University of Queensland. There was nothing in it about race. The set textbook was no help at all. It was the most widely used general history of Australia at the time, frequently reprinted and widely prescribed in universities and senior high schools. It was multi-authored and was in many ways a useful reference, but there was virtually nothing in it about the Aboriginal or Torres Strait Islander people. There was no mention of them in the index. It was, then, representative of the general state of Australian historical scholarship. Did anyone else notice this extraordinary absence, I wondered? So one day I looked up every relevant book review I could find. It had been assessed by many leading scholars. They had numerous things to say, but not one of them had seen what I noticed or, if they did, they didn't think it mattered much.

The small and under-resourced library was little help when I began to look for source material. There were no relevant books and only a few documents. But one was life-changing. It was a pamphlet called *The Way We Civilize*, which was a collection of all the material – editorials, articles and letters – published in *The Queenslander* in 1880.[18] Here was the uncensored, unmediated story of the violent frontier, the frank admission of brutal repression and savage revenge. There was no need to 'rake up' stories of atrocity committed by unscrupulous individuals. Here were articulate correspondents who frankly admitted their role in the killing times and who explained with hard-bitten realism that violence was inescapably part of the whole colonising venture. My understanding of Australian history could never be the same again. There would be a place for retrospective truth-telling, but it had already been done. Was this true of Australia as a whole, I wondered?

I spent ten years seeking to answer that question. I employed the time researching in all the major libraries and archives in Australia as well as in London and Oxford, reading parliamentary debates and printed papers, books, articles, correspondence files, private papers and newspapers, and much else besides. I talked to Aboriginal and Torres Strait Islander people in and around Townsville. No matter what the material was or where it was housed, I found that violence was the dominant message, albeit not the only one by any means. But it was both inescapable and shocking. The newspapers were the most revealing. And there were many of them. The earliest issue I read was in 1803, the latest in 1900. I consulted sixty newspapers from all parts of the country. With some I read a year or two, with others my investigation went on much longer. In all I read through 304 years of newsprint. And it didn't matter where or when the news reports and articles were published, conflict was ever present. It was also taken for granted. It was not as if anyone was surprised that there was frequent fighting out on the ragged edges of the frontier. In some of the papers from the small towns it was close and immediate, with reports only a day or two old, as if from the front. Not everyone approved of the fighting. Certainly, in the big coastal towns correspondents were outraged by the violence. Anger and empathy were woven together in their thoughts and through their words.

When I began my research, the violence was surprising and consequently shocking. But where to begin with trying to understand why it was so common? It was important to try to see it through the eyes of the colonists themselves. They had a variety of explanations. The easiest one was to blame the Aboriginal people themselves. Savages, it was argued, had an innate almost ungovernable propensity to resort to violence. They also had no sense of private property and were natural thieves. But more reflective colonists were able to look beyond these simple nostrums and accord the warriors the respect due to patriots who were defending their homelands against an invader. Other explanations referred to the settlers themselves. The violence was the fault of renegade Europeans, 'unscrupulous individuals', often ex-convicts. Or it was the lawless frontier itself that stripped away the restraints still operating in more settled districts. These were favourite explanations of the disdainful British gentlemen in the Colonial Office and their acolytes in Australia's coastal cities.

The reason for the violence and its actual extent still troubles us. Explanations have moved more towards attributing the blame to the ideas and attitudes of the colonists. They were driven by their racial contempt for their adversaries and, as often as not, were consumed with genocidal passion. Interpretations of this kind have the virtue of being both simple and all embracing, and for some people seem quite satisfying. While simple explanations are often seductive, such complex events occurring over vast distances and across five or six generations cannot be neatly bundled up. But yes, the frontier was commonly, but not always, a very violent place. Far more

Aboriginal Australians were killed than white frontiersmen. Given the almost total absence of white women and children, it was black families that were cut down. The documentary record shows us that, without doubt, there were brutal killers who gloried in their trade and boasted about their exploits. But it is also clear that many men would have preferred to avoid the bloodshed, and were as often as not reluctant conscripts forced by camaraderie to ride out with expeditions to punish the 'niggers' and then return with deeply troubled minds. And for all the forced bravado, there were few people who didn't want a peaceful resolution and an escape from fear and endless, aching anxiety.

What the actual events show us is that the problem goes right back to the beginning. The British government created conditions where violence was unavoidable. It had provided no means to resolve the competing interests without fighting. As we have seen, there was no provision for the negotiation of treaties. It determined that the Aboriginal people were British subjects, but was unable to provide them with the protection of the law. Frontier warfare was predetermined and the convict workforce was predominantly masculine, ensuring that lethal conflict over women was inescapable. When the colonies achieved internal self-government, the three that were responsible for the occupation of northern Australia – South Australia from 1857, Queensland from 1859 and Western Australia from 1890 – showed little interest in tackling traditions of violence already deeply entrenched.

Having come across these forgotten aspects of our history almost by chance, I often thought about the actual scale of the killing. How many people died? It was comparatively easy to count the European dead and record who they were and when, where and how they died. The Aboriginal dead were another matter altogether. Many deaths were never reported. There was no inclination to tell the authorities, and the nearest magistrate or policeman was often many days' ride away. Reports that did appear in the newspapers were likely unreliable, and there was no way of checking them. Night attacks were common and it is unlikely the attackers had any real idea of how many victims they left behind. Clearly, no one knew how many casualties died of their wounds out in the bush. I was fully aware of the scale and the nature of these problems. And yet I felt that given the vast amount of research I had done I had a responsibility to provide the best estimate I could. Looking back now, I realise that I made a number of attempts to do just that, all the while realising that whatever figure I came up with would surprise and shock many people. I was also sure that such truth-telling would be disturbing to a generation of Australians who had grown up believing we had a uniquely peaceful history.

I made my first attempt in an article 'Violence: the Aboriginals, and the Australian historian' published in *Meanjin* in December 1972. I explained that I thought it important to suggest a figure for Aboriginal mortality even if later research proved it wide of the mark. I was not aware of any other such assessment, so I thought I was venturing into unexplored territory. I argued that the Indigenous death rate in frontier conflict was greater than the number of Māori who had died in New Zealand's wars. Queensland alone would have reached that total. I thought that 5000 deaths would be a conservative figure. For Australia as a whole I suggested that 10 000–12 000 deaths 'might be as reasonable a guess as any other, given the present state of our knowledge'.[19]

As my research, and that of numerous colleagues, intensified, the number of assumed deaths on the frontier mounted. By 1978 I estimated that between 800 and 850 settlers and their allies had been killed in Queensland and that it was likely that ten times as many Aboriginal people had met violent deaths.[20] Three years later, in *The Other Side of the Frontier*, I hazarded a figure for the country as a whole, arguing that it was reasonable to suppose that 'at least 20,000 Aborigines were killed as a direct result of conflict with the settlers'.[21] That figure became widely accepted and remained unchallenged until the outbreak of the so-called history wars between 1996 and 2002. I had expected that any estimate would prove to be controversial. The storm of contention was both later coming and more intense than I had expected.

Hostility to revisionist interpretation of the frontier intensified after the High Court's *Mabo* judgment in 1992 and the *Wik* decision four years later. History tucked away in seminar rooms and articles in little-read journals was one thing. History that had subverted the High Court bench was quite another. What had come to be known as 'black-armband' history became a matter of deep concern to Prime Minister John Howard, who came to power in 1996. He believed that the whole of our history was becoming infected with interpretations that challenged the positive story of great national achievements. It undermined young people's patriotism and self-confidence. The fundamental problem was the new history of the frontier. The heroic story of pioneering had been deeply compromised.

The counterattack was led by Keith Windschuttle with his book of 2002 *The Fabrication of Aboriginal History: Volume One, Van Diemen's Land, 1803–1847*. As the title implied, much of the new history was made up or, as how he put it, 'fabricated'. The violence of the frontier was grossly exaggerated and had been done so for overtly political reasons. My estimate of 20 000 deaths was far too high. When his book was launched, one of Windschuttle's prominent supporters declared that the settlement of Australia was so peaceful it was like 'a nun's picnic'.[22]

The book whipped up a storm of controversy.[23] Many people found it worked like a soothing balm. They could now return to an older, comforting interpretation of our history. But the more significant consequence was that it stimulated the emergence of a whole new era in the research of frontier history. Established scholars returned to old research notes. Many new ones emerged. Tasmanian documents were reassessed.[24] But the most significant work was done on the history of northern Australia, particularly Queensland,[25] the Northern Territory and the Kimberley in Western Australia.[26] Within a few years, the weight of evidence was irresistible and essentially unanswerable. Violent conflict erupted everywhere the pastoralists and miners pushed into First Nations' territory. The great improvement in European firearms in the second half of the 19th century meant that the Aboriginal death toll was much higher than in the south, and the number of colonists who suffered was correspondingly smaller. The whole community will eventually have to come to terms with a much higher Indigenous death toll. Twenty thousand is clearly much too small, as we shall see in the next chapter, but that had been apparent for quite some time, Keith Windschuttle's intervention notwithstanding.

Counting bodies does not resolve the bigger questions, however. They are ones that troubled our ancestors. There are many of them. They need to be spelled out. Was violence inevitable or could it have been avoided or at least greatly reduced? Was it an inescapable complement of colonisation? And then there is the overarching question of how much responsibility should be sheeted home to the imperial government. Were the First Nations and the convicts both victims of British imperialism? But even when we have addressed that question, we need to look with clear eyes at our own colonial history. Was Australia's success story built on stolen land, bleaching bones and endless injustice? Were the dead, whatever their number, British subjects who were victims of extrajudicial killing or, to put it more bluntly, murder? Or were they combatants in a rolling but undeclared war? And if it was war, however do we accommodate that fact within our well-established cult of the fallen warrior?

10

QUEENSLAND WAS DIFFERENT

There were two quite distinct phases in the conquest of Australia. The first unfolded in the initial seventy years of colonisation. During that period the British settlers occupied the temperate third of the continent, founding their port cities on the southern coastline, fanning out from there into the well-watered interiors, and establishing farms near the towns and sheep and cattle stations in the broad river valleys. These were the regions of Australia immediately accessible to the sailing ships that rounded the Cape of Good Hope and then ran east before the prevailing winds of the Roaring Forties. They were also the parts of Australia that appeared more familiar to British eyes and sensibilities. The population had reached half a million on the eve of the gold rushes. The Aboriginal peoples had lost control over their ancestral lands and in many cases eked out an impoverished existence on the fringes of society. They were massively outnumbered by their usurpers. Many children were of mixed descent.

In 1850, Victoria was separated from New South Wales and, along with Tasmania and South Australia, was preparing for responsible government, each with its own constitution, parliament and a large measure of self-government. But for much of the previous sixty years, colonial policy had been formulated in Britain and administered by governors answerable to the Colonial Office even when advised by councils of local notables. Their input notwithstanding, policy concerning the First Nations was devised in Britain. Although the colonists vigorously debated the rights and wrongs of what was happening, nothing they could do or say had much effect. Even when humanitarian reforms were introduced, the driving motivation came from overseas and not from the colonial capitals. The chain of moral responsibility for the disastrous results has to be followed back to where the tragic decisions were made, not where they were implemented. The imperial government was aware that in devolving power over the First Nations to the colonists they were also shedding the moral responsibility and the fiduciary duty owed to them. In 1850, Earl Grey, the minister responsible for the Colonial Office, sought to point out the obligations the new governments owed the Aboriginal peoples, for 'In assuming their Territory the settlers in Australia have incurred a moral obligation of the most sacred kind to make all necessary provision for the instruction and improvement of the Natives.'[1]

The second phase played out in the last half of the 19th century and saw the colonists push into the third of the continent that sprawled north of the Tropic of Capricorn. Expansion in that direction had scarcely begun in 1850. There were only 8000 colonists in Queensland, 5000 in Western Australia and almost none in the Northern Territory, where the numbers had only reached 3000 in 1881. Most of the frontiersmen who swept north in the tide of settlement were entering new and unfamiliar territory. There was the constant heat and seasonal humidity, the different pattern of the year from four seasons to just two, the wet and the dry. And those adventurers who came from the south faced the challenge of large and vigorous First Nations who resented the aggressive intrusion.

So from 1859, when Queensland was detached from New South Wales, there was literally a new era of the colonial conquest that, while still underway in the early 20th century, was never as successful nor as complete as what had taken place earlier in the south. But it was an Australian project, not a British imperial one. And that is a most important distinction that is frequently overlooked. The chain of moral responsibility ends in Brisbane and to a lesser degree in Adelaide. The Colonial Office did not grant Western Australia self-government until 1890, and maintained some oversight over Aboriginal policy until 1897. But as a nation, the conquest of the north is our story from which we cannot avert our gaze, and it is one that reached into the early years of the federation. Leaders of the conquest contributed to the drafting of the Constitution and were major figures in the politics and jurisprudence of the fledgling nation. They brought bloodied hands to the affairs of the new federal state.

The colonial governments were far more democratic than the British parliament. There was no hereditary aristocracy and no House of Lords. The franchise was far wider. Manhood suffrage was introduced in South Australia in 1856 and in Queensland in 1872. The courts worked efficiently and fairly for white people, and there was a vigorous growth of a free and independent press. More than thirty newspapers were published in Queensland between 1859 and 1901, from Brisbane and Ipswich in the south to Cooktown and Thursday Island in the north. Not everyone took part in the invasion of the territory of the First Nations. But the saga of settlement, growth and expansion became Queensland's unifying narrative. It was widely shared intellectual property that allowed little space for empathy with the First Nations, which obstructed the ever widening avenues of progress. Humanitarian doubts were not as pervasive as in the larger cities in the south, and it was harder for dissidents to gain a hearing. The first pioneers who came up onto the Darling Downs in the 1840s had arrived with attitudes shaped by the violent conflict experienced in northern New South Wales. They were heavily armed, ready to fight and convinced of their right to wrench land from the traditional owners. Many of the prominent and successful squatters who made that journey north became leaders in the new colony. Above all they 'knew how to handle the blacks'.

The most important tradition that came north with the squatters was that there was a vast rift between the law that had been imposed by the British governors and the customary way of doing things that had emerged from the frontiers. Above all else was the rejection of the pivotal idea that the Aboriginal people were British subjects who were to be provided with all the protection afforded by the common law. The corollary was that killing Indigenous people left one open to a charge of murder and even more generally that it was not legally possible to construe frontier skirmishing as warfare. Both ideas were anathema to frontiersmen and their urban allies and admirers. And they came from all walks of life. A new-world glamour was already arising about the squatters, who had the self-confident swagger of accomplished killers.

Another British judicial legacy successfully contested in the colony was the provision in all pastoral leases that recognised traditional rights of Indigenous landholders to remain on country and have access to water and game and to other sites of importance. It was noted above that these rights existed side by side with the licence accorded to the pastoralists to graze their sheep and cattle on the same stretch of country. There was no getting away from what the law and the lease documents actually said. Earl Grey had explicitly declared that it was illegal to force Aboriginal bands off their country and that it was a matter of great significance as a means of saving them from extermination. Because the pastoral leases were embodied in overriding imperial law, there was nothing colonial legislators could do about them and they were brought back from obscurity in the High Court's *Wik* judgment in 1996. But what the Australians could do with great effectiveness was to simply ignore those Indigenous rights. Aboriginal people were routinely driven off their country whenever a leaseholder chose, and no one did anything about it. They were often shot if they dared walk back onto their land. Many pastoralists may not have known exactly what their lease document said. It seems quite possible that this was also true of the humanitarians who took up the Aboriginal cause. There appears to be no evidence that they ever publicly raised the question of the pastoral leases, let alone brought the matter before the courts.

But Queensland's most egregious departure from the rule of law began when the new government adopted from New South Wales a small police force established to repress Aboriginal resistance in the Northern Rivers district. This native police force had a European commandant, white officers, and Aboriginal troopers recruited from the Murray Valley. It soon became an essential tool in crushing Aboriginal resistance and rode around the outer fringes of the ever expanding frontier until the early years of the 20th century. It was the most distinctive feature of Queensland's pioneering history. It was notorious at the time, and the extensive modern scholarship has done nothing to redeem its evil reputation. There had been a similar force in the Port Phillip region in the 1840s. The small size of what became Victoria allowed for closer official oversight, and the Aboriginal protectors closely watched its operations. Frontier settlers in Western Australia would have developed such a force if left to themselves, but the British government continually vetoed the proposal.

Perhaps the most surprising aspect of the force's history is that administration after administration was able to ignore intense criticism of it from both within Queensland and from the outside world, year after year, and shrug their shoulders at the notoriety that clung to the colony for forty years. Clearly it was seen as irreplaceable, an essential instrument in protecting the frontier settlers. But it was also much cheaper to operate than a normal police force and likely much more efficient. The secrecy that cloaked its operations allowed it to be far more ruthless than any other comparable organisation in Australian history. But it also epitomised recurring aspects of frontier history even while greatly exaggerating them. Ever since Arthur Phillip's abortive punitive expeditions in December 1790, Aboriginal resistance continually challenged the colonists. It broke out practically everywhere. The warriors were hard to find and were far too canny to be easily tracked down. And given the continental stretch of Australia, the only answer seemed to be to exact fierce retribution whenever white men or their property was threatened. It was, as both Phillip and Macquarie had said, a selective use of terror to try to bring recurring conflict to an end with one decisive stroke. Queensland's vast size, the speed of pastoral occupation and the small numbers of white men compared to the Aboriginal population all greatly magnified an enduring problem.

As is probably well known by now, the instructions given to the force didn't change for forty years. The white officers were directed to 'disperse' any large gathering of Aboriginal people. There was never any definition of how many people represented a large gathering, or advice as to whether it mattered if there were men, women or children present, or even if the particular group had been involved in harassing the frontiersmen or their animals. It was an open secret that to disperse was to shoot at. In parliament in 1861, Charles Lilley observed that disperse meant 'nothing but firing into them for that purpose'.[2] Lilley later became the chief justice of the colony. The white officers were allowed an extraordinary amount of discretion. They were able to dispense with all the normal protocols of the criminal law. They didn't arrest suspected warriors. They rarely took prisoners, and if they did they almost always were shot while 'trying to escape'. There were no trials and no inquests. Queensland did not have the prisons that were widely used in Western Australia at much the same time. Photos from there of chained Aboriginal people are distressing to modern eyes, but in Queensland the solution to the same problem was to shoot down men, women and children in the bush and to burn their bodies to destroy incriminating cadavers.

Among a vast body of evidence about the Queensland native police, perhaps the most telling is a speech in the parliament in 1880 by John Douglas while making an unsuccessful appeal for the establishment of a royal commission into the force. Douglas was a prominent member of the House of Assembly. He had been in the parliament since 1863, a minister between 1866 and 1869, and premier between 1879 and 1881. He knew what he was talking about. The force he observed had 'no foundation in law whatever, and yet it had been perpetuated from year to year'. Its constitution was 'very abnormal and not in accordance with either military or civil law'. At the present time, he declared,

> they did nothing else but shoot them down whenever they
> could get at them. That was the sole function of the native
> police. As far as could be judged from their instructions
> and practices, they were chiefly kept as a military force in
> dispersing the natives when they congregated, and patrolling
> districts to drive the blacks into positions where they could
> not come into contact with the European settlers.[3]

The attempt to establish a commission failed, not solely because the opponents of the proposition disagreed with

Douglas but rather through an awareness of what infamous testimony would likely be aired. Arthur Palmer rejected the proposal. He was one of the politicians who had lived out on the frontier. In public he defended the force. In private it was a different matter. In a letter written in 1882, he expressed sympathy for the 'unfortunate blacks the way they are treated'. They were driven from their country and 'whenever they are seen by the Native Police the rule has been to shoot them'.[4] Palmer had been premier for five years in the early 1870s and the minister responsible for the police between 1879 and 1881. Like Douglas, he knew what he was talking about.

The evidence is incontrovertible. The main purpose of native police force was to kill Aboriginal people in sufficient numbers to terrorise them into submission and to prevent them from attacking the colonists and their property. The force did this for many years over a vast area. It has been obvious to historians for a long time that a great many men, women and children died as a consequence. How many has been difficult to calculate. The whole point about the force was that it operated in secret. The detachments patrolled remote areas and moved forward as the frontier of settlement progressed. The scandals that were exposed were often a consequence of indiscretions by the officers when they took action too close to townships and to potential witnesses. The bodies of victims were usually incinerated. The sub-inspectors, as the officers were called, sent monthly reports to the Police Commissioner's Office in Brisbane. This vast trove of information was apparently destroyed, possibly in the 1930s.

But meticulous research by Queensland historians Ray Evans and Robert Ørsted-Jensen has found a sample of the monthly reports that ended up in the papers of other government departments and they have used these to make an estimate of the death toll. Drawing on the work of Jonathan Richards, they began by counting those things that could be enumerated, including the number of police camps and the duration of active occupation. There had been eighty-four camps in operation between 1859 and 1897, covering an aggregate period of 596 years. They then counted the number of patrols conducted by each detachment and arrived at a reasonable minimum figure for the whole colony over forty or so years. In all, there were over 7000 patrols. They assumed that the 111 monthly reports that had survived were, by their very nature, a random sample, as were the number of reported deaths. In forty years they calculated that the native police killed over 40 000 Aboriginal men, women and children. It was literally a shocking figure. Evans and Ørsted-Jensen observed:

Such estimations no doubt appear radical and iconoclastic – even extreme. They certainly detonate the consensual 20,000 Australia-wide figure, allegedly tabulated over 140 years of conflict … Yet the methodology employed has been uniformly conservative throughout. Each considered estimate has been assiduously pruned and discreetly diminished. This is a cautious, minimal assessment rather than one that is excessive or capriciously assembled.[5]

But parties of settlers also took the field against the Aboriginal people. Many such attacks were recorded in one way or another. Ørsted-Jensen has compiled a list of 275 of them. He has found 113 actual accounts provided by participants or witnesses. The average number of reported deaths was just over eight. Conservatively extrapolating the known figures to 258 private attacks suggests a total of over 20 000 violent deaths at private hands. The authors observed that it is a feasible figure 'given the settlers' notorious reticence in reporting their dispersal activities as well as a high level of assault …'.[6] Bringing the two sets of figures together, Evans and Ørsted-Jensen estimate that the overall death rate amounted to between 61 000 and 62 000 in 6000 attacks. It is truly an awesome conclusion.

The two historians realise the gravity of their scholarship, commenting that:

> We are fully aware of the implications of our findings. We have been incrementally conducting this research during a time when conscientious historians have been pilloried for even suggesting that a range of serious massacres once occurred in Australia. We are acutely sensitive to the wider denialist mood in some sections of Australian society and its mainstream media. And so we proceed with caution and conservative assessment, even as we wear the derisively placed 'black armband' with conviction. We research, calculate and write in order to return to history the full ledger of those who, long ago, died protecting their sovereignty, their cultures, their homelands and

their peoples; but whose deaths were more often hidden than acknowledged by a society that made furtiveness its watchword. Our allegiance is towards identifying, as best we can, historical precision and accuracy, however disturbing this may be ...[7]

What needs to be added to this statement is that the two authors have an unrivalled knowledge of Queensland's historical records. Evans has worked on them for fifty years, ever since he wrote an honours thesis that was one of the first ventures into revisionist historiography. But their work also rests on a much larger body of research, which can be found in theses, articles and books by a cohort of perhaps twenty or so writers who, between them, have transformed our understanding of Queensland history. So the estimates made by Evans and Ørsted-Jensen have to be taken very seriously indeed. Once they are as widely accepted as they should be, Australian history will never be the same again. It will no longer be possible to hide the bodies or skirt around the violence that was required to quell the resistance of the First Nations during the conquest of northern Australia.

But what then? What effect will this scholarship have on the national story? Perhaps more particularly, how do we accommodate the slaughter? It is necessary to remember that, legally speaking, the Aboriginal people were British subjects. That was beyond doubt. So are we dealing with extrajudicial killing carried out on a massive scale over many years? To put it more bluntly, was it murder? If so, what does this say about the legal system and the rule of law that we are often told was part of our precious British inheritance? And to make matter's worse, only a handful of people were ever arrested, charged, tried and sentenced for murder in all those blood-stained years. Why did things go so wrong? These were not mere blemishes, or a few scars, or a case of mismanagement. They were deep and critical wounds that have still not fully healed. How could it be otherwise?

There are other ways to understand the violence. Was it a product of war? Distinctive indeed but war nonetheless? Like residents in the southern colonies before them, the Queenslanders referred to war in speeches and in letters to the newspapers, and we can reasonably assume in innumerable private conversations. In a statement to the new parliament in 1861, John Watts declared that 'the people of this colony must be considered to be, as they always have been, at open war with the Aborigines'.[8] Elsewhere they were said to be engaged in an actual state of warfare, a kind of open war, guerrilla warfare, a secret war to the knife. *The Queenslander* declared in 1879 that 'we are today at open war with every tribe of wild blacks on the frontiers of settlement'.[9] Victims of the native police were 'shot in battle',[10] a parliamentary select committee was informed in 1861, on what an ex-officer of the force called 'the unrecorded battlefields of Queensland'.[11] The editor of the *Rockhampton Bulletin* declared in 1870 that,

> No way of treating them, except as belligerents when they
> commit outrages, has yet been found efficacious in the
> back tracks. They may be tolerated and treated kindly
> so long as they refrain from mischievous acts, but when

they rob, steal, or murder, they must be treated as enemies
of the state and shot down with as little compunction
as soldiers shoot each other in battles amongst civilised
men. This is a deplorable necessity we admit. But is it
more deplorable than the practice in modern civilised
warfare?[12]

Comparisons were often made between frontier conflict
and other imperial battlefields, and between expenditure on
external defence and the inadequate provision for the settlers in contention with the First Nations. A correspondent in
The Queenslander in 1879 argued that: 'We have not grudged
a large outlay on national defence with but a very doubtful
prospect of foreign attack', so why did the government 'stint
the funds necessary for the repression of the enemy within our
gates?'[13] Writing to the same paper eight years later, a settler
on the Atherton Tableland pointed out that while there were
thousands, 'that can be spent in Defence Forces, to protect the
inhabitants of this country from invisible, perhaps imaginary,
but for certain distant enemies; but we cannot afford to keep
an efficient body of police to keep in check the enemy we have
at our door, the enemy of every day, the one that slowly but
surely robs and impoverishes us'.[14]

But while colonists debated whether frontier conflict had
the seriousness and gravity of warfare, there could be no such
uncertainty among the First Nations. It was an unimagina-
ble catastrophe. Not many human societies have suffered so
severely. The fighting itself was viewed very differently on
the other side of the frontier. What the colonists thought of as

brief punitive expeditions may have caused far greater havoc than they appreciated. Family groups were torn apart, kinship networks were severely disrupted, and when elders were killed much of the collective knowledge and wisdom was lost forever. And the trauma was magnified because it was often the case that all the rituals surrounding death had to be abandoned. Aboriginal communities had not traditionally lived in peace, but intertribal violence was usually contained. Revenge killing was commonplace but it was usually proportionate. One death was answered by another one. But it was this custom of tit-for-tat killing that the colonists could not tolerate. And that tradition goes back to Phillip and Macquarie. So when white men were killed the response, almost everywhere, was to react totally disproportionately in order to 'teach them a lesson they will never forget' and bring resistance to an end with one sharp shock.

What the Europeans saw as scattered, intermittent skirmishing, and still do today, was experienced very differently among the First Nations. The conflict took the shape and the timing it did because of the structure of Aboriginal society. They did not fight as part of a general comprehensive campaign. They resisted the invaders when they entered their own country. Each nation fought back in its own way, adopting their own tactics and finally finding some way to accommodate themselves to the ongoing presence of the white men and their animals. There were, in effect, many small, fierce, destructive wars. And wars they were, because they were about both sovereignty over a small national territory and the ownership and control of property. The warfare was also remarkably widespread, because the First Nations occupied the whole continent with a far wider distribution of population than was true of the colonists' Australia then or, indeed, even now. It was inevitable that war would eventually break out wherever and whenever the colonists thrust their way deeper into First Nations Australia. It was inimitably Australian war, shaped by our geography and demography and the nature of the ancient Indigenous society. We have only begun to come to terms with the fact that this war belongs to us all.

How do we secure it as part of our national history? Clearly numbers matter to us as a nation. We carefully account for every Australian who died in our many overseas wars. That is why the generation-long attempt to estimate the numbers killed in frontier conflict has continued and at the same time has whipped up such controversy and hostility. It matters to us and so it should. So the new estimates of 60 000 dead in Queensland alone cannot be deftly set aside. They inevitably lead on to considerations of the overall national total. Evans has suggested that the figure could be as high as 115 000.[15] It is clearly the case that Queensland was different. In Western Australia the imperial government acted to restrain the more belligerent characteristic of the northern march, and that was to some extent true of the colonisation of southern Australia. The weapons available to the frontiersmen made them far more efficient killers in the last thirty years of the 19th century. So the Evans calculation may be too high but perhaps not all that much so. Even if we consider a figure of 100 000, it dramatically changes the nature of the national narrative. Such a startling denouement cannot be easily assimilated into long-known plots. That figure is equal to all the Australians who have died in all our much storied wars overseas.

Truth-telling is now more important than ever. What has been a personal choice is now a national imperative. We need to return to the tough-minded honesty of our ancestors. Men like the pioneer of the North Queensland town of Bowen, who wrote to the local paper the *Port Denison Times* in 1869 admitting that 'We know that our own town at least had its foundations cemented in blood.'[16] Denialism is no longer a viable option. A wall of scholarship built by many hands over the last fifty years stands in the way. So too does the High Court. In the *Mabo* judgment, the bench overturned 200 years of precedent and declared that in 1788 the First Nations were both the occupiers and owners of their traditional land. So regardless of how the frontier wars were fought, no matter how small and seemingly inconsequential, they had to be about the ownership and control of property over vast stretches of country. A whole continent was in contention. The stakes could not have been higher. And the war was fought in Australia and it was about Australia. Is there any reason why we should not come to see that this was our most important war? Our overseas engagements, no matter how significant, were about strategic objectives decided elsewhere. Our enemies were chosen for us. We were told where to fight, when to fight and how to fight. If it came to a point, we could have avoided these wars. That was not an option when it came to frontier conflict. That was an insight expressed by many people in all parts of the country during the first century of colonisation, one that was progressively eschewed in the 20th century.

It is not just the number of Aboriginal deaths that must be remembered but the heroism of their many small wars in defence of their homelands, their customs and traditions, their accustomed way of life and their very survival as a people. How is it possible that this desperate fight has not been recognised in a society obsessed with the sacrifice of the fallen warrior and that has revered the iconic phrase 'Lest We Forget'? What is wrong with us? The Aboriginal people were British subjects in theory at least, they became full citizens by the 1960s, and the overwhelming expectation is that they will be both partners in loyalty to the state and members of the national community. How can we non-Indigenous Australians not see their war dead as heroes and patriots when they died both on and for our soil, not for someone else's country far away? The question that forces its way into all such discussions is are the people of the First Nations the countrymen and -women of non-Indigenous Australians or not? Was their fight also the nation's fight? And that leads inescapably to the question of how war is remembered and how it is commemorated.

II

REMEMBERING THE DEAD

Historical research of the last twenty years has confirmed the central importance of the killing times. They lasted far longer and were much more deadly than generations of Australians were led to believe. For many years the truth was either deftly avoided or consciously suppressed. Aboriginal families kept alive their own memories of those terrible times, even if they were not necessarily aware of the broader national story. A pioneer Queensland pastoralist who had worked for years with Indigenous stockmen came to appreciate the continuing legacy of the violent early years, or what he termed 'the remembrance of the blood red dawn of their civilisation'. He was continually frustrated by 'the traditions of the past – the hereditary hatred of the whites through the butchery of their ancestors'.[1] Once anthropologists and linguists began to work in First Nations communities in the 1930s and 1940s, they too learnt how vigorously alive were memories of historical violence. They should perhaps have known more about it but often didn't. Their education had let them down.

The violence, the 'line of blood', was well known in colonial society, as abundant evidence in earlier chapters has demonstrated. It had been discussed and argued about from the earliest years in New South Wales and Tasmania. The central points of contention still confront us. Was it an inescapable companion of colonisation? Was it a case of forced appropriation or none at all? Were all the colonists, including those with no experience of the frontier, complicit by remaining in Australia? Did the new societies bear a collective moral burden? Or was it necessary to distinguish the culpability of free settlers from that of the convicts and the Australian-born children? 'This right to Australia is a sore subject with many of the British settlers', a Victorian pioneer noted in the 1840s, 'and they strive to satisfy their consciences in various ways.'[2] At much the same time, the South Australian settler Francis Dutton thought that the claims of the blacks were 'superior to ours', although his contemporaries were 'too eager on all occasions, by casuistical reasonings, to persuade ourselves that such is not the case'.[3] The Aboriginal question 'gave rise to more argument' than any other matter in Queensland in the 1860s according to the editor of the *Rockhampton Bulletin*.[4] Running close to the colonial debate about the morality of settlement was the unavoidable question of frontier conflict. Was it a form of warfare even if of quite a distinctive kind? Or were the pioneer settlers murderers? Were they heroic pathfinders or criminals? There were very few court cases where such questions might have been assessed and therefore publicised. On the other hand, war and homicide were matters widely understood, each with their own place in the popular mind. So there was no consensus, no resolution that has been passed down to us. We have to resolve the matter ourselves.

As we have seen earlier, there were always settlers who opted for warfare as the way out of the moral quandary of colonisation. And perhaps more to the point many of the military men who lived and worked in New South Wales and Tasmania talked openly of war and many of them were career officers with battle experience. Many of them had served in the Peninsula War and had first-hand knowledge of the guerrilla campaign waged by Spanish peasants against the French army. It is not surprising therefore that many of the historians who have rewritten the history of frontier conflict over the last forty or so years have followed in their wake. More to the point is that since at least 1990, Australia's professional war historians have both accepted and promoted the idea that frontier conflict must be considered alongside Australia's overseas wars. But that can only be the start of a significant transformation in the way we think about both the frontiersmen and the warriors of the First Nations who confronted them all over the continent. Rigorous truth-telling will be of critical importance here, but that can only be part of the required transformation. The telling must be heard and treated with gravity. Changes in traditional accounts of national history will have to be accepted. Above all, we must bring together the ways we think about and commemorate the two forms of national war-making ... the many overseas campaigns on the one hand and the war fought in Australia for the ownership and control of the continent on the other. The truth-telling will have achieved its ultimate purpose when Australian children are able to consider that the long-running and widespread conflict that accompanied Australian life for 140 years was arguably our most important war.

But how can two such disparate narratives be spliced together? It will clearly take time and will need steady and persistent commitment. Many small threads will have to be engaged. Complexity will have to replace simple sagas of heroic settlement. For instance, few people appreciate that Aboriginal people participated from the earliest years in the outward thrust of the frontier. The first expeditions that pushed out into the interior were invariably accompanied by Aboriginal escorts who acted as guides and diplomats. They were able to find their way across country, discover water, track straying horses, hunt and gather food. They could quickly construct temporary shelters and simple bark rafts to ford rivers. Their value was so obvious that it became a settled custom for expeditions, both private and official, to recruit young men and women to act as valued auxiliaries. When the squatters surged out into the interior of New South Wales Aboriginal people went with them and quickly developed the skills that made them valued and competent stockmen and -women. Children, often enough kidnapped, were taken along as personal servants and eventually sexual partners. Once the vast savannah lands of the tropical north were occupied, local Aboriginal people became the mainstay of the workforce, given the scarcity, cost and unreliability of white labour. They were an essential component of the successful establishment of the northern pastoral industry and, consequently, the principal claim the settler Australians could make to prove they were in effective occupation of as much as a quarter of the continent.

The same skills made young Aboriginal men ideal troopers for native police forces in Victoria, New South Wales and particularly Queensland. Their bushcraft was essential to the success of the northern force in crushing the resistance of the First Nations over a vast area of the colony. They were also much cheaper to maintain than a comparable force of European troopers. There seems to be no precise record of the number of Aboriginal young men who served in the force. In his history of the native police, *The Secret War*, Jonathan Richards listed just over 250 white officers who spent varying periods of time out in the field.[5] But he provided no estimate of the equivalent number of Indigenous troopers. There must have been hundreds and possibly as many as a thousand. The conclusions that follow from this are compelling. The troopers almost certainly killed more Aboriginal people than the settlers. In total, they may have been responsible for up to a quarter of all deaths in the frontier wars all over Australia. This too has to be part of our truth-telling.

The response of many people when this matter is raised is to express amazement that the troopers could shoot their own people and assume they must have been coerced into killing. But the critical point is that the idea that the First Nations were members of one race or one people was a European one and had little bearing on the situation on the ground. The young troopers were invariably campaigning far from their own homeland in country previously unknown among people foreign to them. And the locals were people to be feared. If the troopers were caught away from their detachment they would almost certainly have been killed, and this kept them together as much as the discipline imposed by white officers.

So whether as paramilitary troopers, workers, trackers,

guides, servants or sexual partners, many hundreds of Aboriginal Australians were participants in the outward thrust of the frontier. The implication is inescapable. Many Indigenous families have ancestors who were pioneers in the precise meaning of that term, both black and white, whether recognised and acknowledged or not.

Truth-telling allows us to weave new stories and to make old ones richer while, at the same time, more complex. This is particularly true when it comes to our understanding of frontier warfare. The common view is that the Aboriginal peoples were, for much of the time, passive victims of European brutality. The course of events was determined by the frontiersmen. They had the upper hand in almost all situations. They were the aggressors and their animus provoked and then consummated the violence. Such ideas have been with us for a long time. They help explain the one-time common view that the Aboriginal peoples were quite unable to put up a spirited resistance of the kind seen in New Zealand and North America, that they were 'pathetically helpless' in their response to the invaders of their homelands. They neither evoked fear nor earned respect and so were noticed in national history as no more than a melancholy anthropological footnote. Such opinions, common among professional historians until the 1960s, underpinned the idea that we had a uniquely peaceful history. Since then, as we have seen, the violence of the frontier has flooded back into the national story. But the overwhelming idea of Aboriginal people as victims of irresistible violence has lived on as a powerful political weapon, readily mobilised to assault the conscience of white Australia. But as is often the case, good politics makes bad history.

A few days' research among the documentary records of the colonies would dispel these ideas. It was understood at the time that white fear was overwhelmingly important. The brave frontiersmen were terrified of the Aboriginal people. The evidence for this will be found everywhere. A *Sydney Morning Herald* journalist who toured North Queensland in the 1880s considered the question of whether killing was 'ever done wantonly ... in an unprovoked manner and for pure satisfaction of killing'. He concluded that 'mere wanton slaughter would be unknown if the natives were not feared so much'.[6] Some years later, on the other side of the continent, the government resident at Roebourne reported that the 'fears of whites are more the cause of disorder than the aggression of blacks'.[7] This should come as no surprise. In most frontier districts the invading force was spread very thin and became progressively thinner north of Capricorn. The small parties were almost everywhere outnumbered by resident bands. They were in country they knew little about. It looked, felt and smelt dangerously exotic. They had no maps and had no idea where Aboriginal parties periodically disappeared to. The people they were displacing had a profound knowledge of their own land. They were in many cases taller, stronger and better nourished than the Europeans, who got by on a very limited diet. And they were hunters trained from childhood. They could track the intruders and stalk them without being seen or heard, and throw their spears with lethal force and accuracy. There was every reason to fear them. Guns were important, particularly late in the 19th century when men on the frontier carried revolvers and high-powered repeating rifles. But it was the horse that had tipped the balance in the invaders' favour. Their power, speed and endurance made all the difference on the vast open plains of inland Australia.

When speaking in their own defence, frontiersmen insisted that they acted in response to Aboriginal aggression. A typical argument was advanced by the editor of the *Hodgkinson Mining News* who wrote in 1877: 'It is not the rule that the white men are the aggressors. The first settlers came peaceably onto the land they had got by right from the Crown, and no sooner had they done so than the hostilities of the natives compel them to adopt not merely defensive but offensive measures.'[8] It was special pleading but there is no doubt the frontiersmen, like invaders anywhere, would have preferred to achieve a bloodless usurpation.

The editor's comment nudges us, however, towards an enhanced understanding of the frontier wars. It was Aboriginal resistance that determined where and when conflict broke out and for how long it lasted. And that was clearly the result of innumerable political decisions, made often at band level, about how to respond to the white men. Initially there was a choice of attempting to accommodate the intruders, avoiding them altogether or spying on them in order to gather information about them. The fateful decision to begin forceful resistance often took some time. It may have begun with a compelling desire to carry out a revenge mission aimed at a particular individual for what would have been a crime in traditional society – the kidnapping and rape of a kinswoman for instance.

From that point on, violence spiralled out of control.

Attacks on vulnerable white men were often combined with the killing of sheep, cattle and horses; the burning of huts and crops; and the pillaging of undefended camp sites. The fighting continued until the Aboriginal bands decided that the cost they were paying was too high. Once again there must have been intense and urgent debate about how to bring the merciless killing to an end. And even then, the question of how to negotiate a capitulation must have occupied time and thought. But everywhere, sooner or later, the survivors were, in the victors' words, 'let in' to pastoral stations, mining camps or rudimentary townships. Not everyone was willing to surrender, and small parties of what the white men called *myalls* continued to live independently in remote areas of their homeland.

Clearly, Australian history has come a long way in understanding the frontier wars and appreciating the heroic struggles of many small nations. To advance along this path any further we can once again consult perceptive and sympathetic colonists. The explorer Edward Eyre was one of the people who was able to look beyond the conventional view that the warriors were dangerous but lacking martial virtue. He observed that:

> It has been said, and is generally believed, that the natives
> are not courageous. There could not be a greater mistake
> ... nor do I hold it to be any proof that they are cowards,
> because they dread or give way before Europeans and their
> fire-arms. So unequal a match is no criterion of bravery,
> and yet even thus, among natives, who were labouring
> under the feelings, naturally produced by seeing a race

they were unacquainted with, and weapons that dealt
death as if by magic, I have seen many instances of an open
manly intrepidity of manner and bearing, and a proud
unquailing glance of eye, which instinctively stamped
upon my mind the conviction that the individuals before
me were very brave men.[9]

From an admiration of Aboriginal bravery it required a
further step to regard the warriors as heroic patriots defending their homelands, although that was one too demanding for
most colonists. It required an even-handed approach difficult
to sustain in times of conflict and that threatened to undermine the legal and moral foundations on which the Australian
colonies rested. Much discussion has already established that
the British claim to both property and sovereignty depended
on the view that the continent was a *terra nullius* where the
local inhabitants ranged over the land without having any
deep attachment to it. They could simply move on to alternative territory. Any spot would be suitable.

It was the war in Tasmania in the 1820s that swept all
of these preconceptions aside and produced one of colonial
Australia's most provocative manifestoes. It was printed in a
Launceston newspaper at the very end of five years of conflict.
The author 'J.E.', assumed to be the young surveyor James
Erskine Calder, posed what he called some solemn questions
about the islands' Aboriginal peoples. He declared: 'We are at
war with them: they look upon us as enemies – as invaders –
as their oppressors and persecutors – they resist our invasion.
They have never been subdued, therefore they are not rebel-

lious subjects, but an injured nation, defending in their own way, their rightful possessions, which have been torn from them by force.' Given the time that it was written that was provocative enough. But J.E. followed the logic of his position much further arguing:

> What we call their crime is what in a white man we should call patriotism. Where is the man amongst ourselves who would not resist an invading enemy; who would not avenge the murder of his parents, the ill-usage of his wife and daughters, and the spoliation of all his earthly goods, by a foreign enemy, if he had an opportunity? He who would not do so, would be scouted, execrated, nay executed as a coward and a traitor; while he who did would be immortalized as a patriot. Why then shall we deny the same feelings to the Blacks? How can we condemn as a crime in these savages what we should esteem as a virtue in ourselves? Why punish a black man with death for doing that which a white man would be executed for not doing?[10]

They were challenging questions then. They remain so today.

I came across J.E.'s letter years ago and have used it in several books. I have also read it to audiences in many parts of Australia. In almost all cases people have found it a complete surprise. They are amazed that a colonist would publish such an enlightened letter almost 200 years ago. They correctly assess that his questions still confront and challenge us. Can we, by which I mean Australia as a nation, regard the

First Nations' warriors as patriots? Can we immortalise their heroic defence of their homelands? We have a great deal of experience when it comes to remembering and commemorating our citizens who have died in conflict. We probably do it more thoroughly than almost any other nation. No expense is spared. The phrase 'Lest We Forget' is surrounded by a sacred penumbra. So there is no doubt we know how to immortalise our fallen patriots. But do we want to allow the heroes of the First Nations to join the chosen ones? Do we want to extend to them the honours we award to the war dead from all our overseas engagements? Do we want to honour them with a place in the nation's pantheon? Do we want to share the honours we have hitherto preserved for our warriors who fought on foreign soil? Spend as much on the project? See it as a national priority? If the answer is yes, what would be required?

Djon Mundine's burial poles were a response to the fact that memorials to our overseas wars can be found all over the continent, even in the smallest and most isolated villages. In his book *Sacred Places*, Ken Inglis estimated that there are more than 4000 war memorials of one kind or another.[11] And then there are the tens of thousands of graves cared for by the War Graves Commission in Australia and many places overseas. We also keep an accurate count of our war dead and still search for the bodies of our servicemen and -women buried in unmarked graves. If they are found we rebury them with full military honours. During the carnival of First World War commemoration we witnessed between 2014 and 2018, old monuments all over the country were refurbished and avenues of honour replanted. A new museum costing $100 million was built in northern France to commemorate the achievements of the AIF in Europe during the First World War. Meanwhile the Australian War Memorial had achieved an unparalleled place in national life. Visiting schoolchildren are taught that it is where they must go to understand what it means to be an Australian. It is increasingly used for solemn national ceremonies. It is now described by the director of the institution as the 'soul of the nation',[12] a view endorsed by Defence Minister Linda Reynolds, who told a Senate Estimates Committee that the memorial embodied 'the soul and the psyche of Australians'.[13] The government has recently granted it half a billion dollars for a highly controversial building program.

The memorial's apotheosis has been achieved during the years when many aspects of Australian history were transformed and in particular our new understanding of the magnitude of the frontier wars. But rather than embrace the new historiography, the memorial has turned its back on it, despite the highly relevant research and writing of many of the Canberra-based war historians some of whom have actually worked inside the institution. The reason for this recalcitrance has never been convincingly outlined. The most common explanation is that while frontier conflict has been accepted as part of the national story, it should come under the aegis of the National Museum rather than the War Memorial. Australia's two stories of war were, it seems, to be kept perpetually apart and unequal by a form of curatorial apartheid. From a national perspective, the War Memorial's implicit disrespect for the warriors of the First Nations represents a case of profound moral failure. It has let us all down. It was made worse by a parallel political failure as a consequence of the complete lack of interest in the subject from all sides of the federal parliament. Either the politicians didn't care or perhaps they felt the memorial was above criticism. And the problem could have been resolved so easily. One formal ceremony would have woven the two traditions together. The placing of a tomb for the unknown warrior in the heart of the memorial next to the grave of the unknown soldier would have been an event of immense national importance, a symbol of respect, inclusion and reconciliation. What a difference that would have made to the way we feel about ourselves!

There seems little chance now that this will ever happen. We will have to persist with two separate stories of war. The inescapable implication is that the nation itself is deeply divided, its soul bifurcated and located in different places. But if the two histories are to be told in different ways and in distinctive institutions, they must be given equal resources to not only continue the truth-telling, called for in the Uluru Statement from the Heart, but to enable the truth to be proclaimed and illustrated in a compelling way. The call must be: 'If not inclusion then equality.' What is clearly required is a new national museum dedicated to the frontier wars and supported with the same level of funding that is received by the War Memorial. It will be expensive, but if $100 million can be lavished on building a museum dedicated to a few years of fighting in France, that is the least that should be expected to establish an institution here in Australia dedicated to the story of the conflict that was experienced in all parts of the continent over 140 years. The new institution could then provide advice and encouragement to regional organisations to consider ways to research and commemorate the war fought within their own traditional boundaries. Not every community would necessarily respond, but the variety of the chosen manner and form would likely provide an exhilarating experience for locals and visitors alike. In some places the descendants of the white pioneers might be invited to participate in the commemoration. They might or might not wish to be included.

Museums and monuments are important instruments to both remember the past and to engage in truth-telling. They have, as a result, often been immersed in controversy. But historical reputations have also been strongly contested in many places in recent years. It is time to consider the way we currently view public figures implicated in the killing times.

12

THE CONSEQUENCES
OF TRUTH-TELLING

Truth-telling has consequences. So too does reinterpretation of history. Controversy is whipped up and the coals of dormant culture wars are fanned back into life. Reputations are called into question; status is reassigned. Old certainties are challenged and new ways of thinking about the past broadcast to the world. These developments have been apparent in many countries. They are clearly related to the complex story of decolonisation that unfolded during the second half of the 20th century and the concomitant rebellion against the racial ideas that had for so long provided white people with unearned certainty and justification for repression and exploitation. In both South and North America, the legacy of slavery continues to stimulate debate about reparation and moral culpability and, as in Australia and New Zealand, the destructive impact of colonisation is an abiding concern. A common response is to reconsider the history of European settlement and replace the explorers and pioneers with the men and women of the First Nations, celebrating their resistance and resilience.

In the Americas, the historical standing of Columbus has been under siege for some time. In the United States the struggle centres on Columbus Day, 12 October, a national holiday since the 1930s. Over the last twenty years, individual states, starting with South Dakota, have renamed the holiday Indigenous Peoples' Day. Ten States have followed suit, along with at least fifty-five major cities and many local districts. Similar developments are taking place in Latin America. In 2015, a statue of Columbus that had stood for many years in a prominent plaza in Buenos Aires was replaced by one of Juana Azurduy de Padilla, a Mestizo woman warrior who had fought the Spaniards in the wars of independence. The choice of leaders of the resistance to the Spanish forces as national heroes is now widespread in South and Central America, including Cuba, Venezuela, Bolivia, Peru, Chile, Puerto Rico, Hispaniola and Guatemala.

In Peru the husband-and-wife team of Túpac Amaru and Micaela Bastidas are national heroes whose names appear on streets, plazas and buildings. There are large statues of Amaru in Lima and Cuzco, and his face is reproduced on banknotes, coins and stamps. Chile gives comparable recognition to Caupolicán, one of the principal leaders of the Mapuche people's resistance to the Spanish forces. His statue has commanded the view from a rocky outcrop, Santa Lucíía Hill, in the centre of Santiago since 1910, and a town, a theatre, streets and parks are named after him. Clearly the history of Australia is very different from that of the Latin American republics. There have been few attempts to accord Indigenous warriors the national respect paid to the men and women who fought the Spanish settlers and their armed forces. However, in March 2018 the Western Australian government opened a major new development in the centre of Perth and named it Yagan Square after the Whadjuk Noongar warrior.

Statues and other monuments have been at the centre of debate in many countries in recent years. The United States has seen intense disagreement over the present status and future of the hundreds of monuments in the south commemorating the Civil War. Statues of Confederate general Robert E Lee and Jefferson Davis, the president of the Confederacy, have been removed in a few cities, leading to angry debate and in Charlottesville, Virginia, to violent demonstrations. Many southerners argue that whatever one thinks about the legacy of the Civil War and of slavery, the monuments are an integral part of their historical memory and represented a cause for which tens of thousands of their ancestors were willing to die. On the other hand, many Americans believe that the statues give retrospective validation to the shameful history of slavery. Clearly that is a subject that never goes away and has been more in need of truth-telling than almost any other. But there is a deep public commitment to official involvement. The National Museum of African American History and Culture opened in Washington DC in 2017. The following year the Legacy Museum opened in Montgomery, Alabama, with a special section devoted to more than 4000 lynchings carried out between 1877 and 1950. As with all such institutions, the displays provide a manner of truth-telling that is impossible to ignore, leaving many locals 'quietly seething' and insisting that the community should 'let sleeping dogs lie'.[1] At much the same time, San Francisco was debating the future of a statue, *Early Days*, that had been in place for

124 years, depicting 'a native American on his back, defeated, a Catholic priest above him pointing to the heavens and an anglicized vaquero bestriding the scene in triumph'. It was removed in September 2018 amid inevitable controversy and projected legal challenges.[2]

While the Americans have been in ongoing dispute about statues of confederate leaders, South Africa debated the historical legacy of Cecil Rhodes. At the centre of the dispute was a statue of Rhodes that had stood in the University of Cape Town since 1934. It had come to be seen as an unacceptable symbol of the perpetuation of white racism and privilege. After a short and assertive campaign, the university's senate voted to remove the statue, which was accomplished in early April 2015, just three weeks after the protest began. Clearly Rhodes had few friends, even fewer defenders. How the mighty had fallen! But the 'Rhodes Must Fall' campaign spread to other universities, where the movement widened out to demand a much more general 'decolonisation of education'. Universities in both Britain and the United States moved in the same direction. There was a failed attempt at Oxford to have a bust of Rhodes removed from a college façade, but activists recently returned to the streets with renewed demands.[3] Cambridge University announced the establishment of a research project to determine the extent to which it had contributed to, benefited from or challenged slavery and the slave trade. The decision was met with widespread criticism.[4] Glasgow University has raised 20 million pounds to set up a joint development research centre with the University of the West Indies after calculating the benefits it had received directly and indirectly from the slave trade.[5] Statues of slave traders have been removed in Bristol and London.[6]

Many of the older and more prestigious American universities have been engaged in a mission to investigate historic ties to slavery. This often involved wealthy benefactors whose fortunes derived from the trade and whose names were still acknowledged. Slaves had worked in a number of institutions and Georgetown University, the Jesuit institution in Washington DC, had both owned and sold slaves. Harvard Law School scrapped a family crest of a slave-trading family that had funded the first chair in law. In 2018 to mark the bicentenary, a commemorative plaque in honour of the slaves was unveiled by the university's president. Elsewhere, artworks were commissioned, lectures funded and further research commissioned. A special committee at Brown University raised questions that troubled many kindred institutions, observing: 'How do we reconcile those elements of our past that are gracious and honorable with those that provoke grief and horror? What responsibilities, if any, rest upon us in the present as inheritors of this mixed legacy?'[7]

Many of these developments in the Americas, South Africa and Britain were not widely reported in Australia, but their relevance to our own experience with truth-telling is obvious. There is the question of what responsibility rests on the shoulders of those who inherit a troubled legacy. Almost universally that very large question has emerged: should societies face up to and reconcile with their past or is it better to look to the future and let sleeping dogs lie? These questions were thrust upon an often reluctant Australian public when in August 2017 statues in Sydney's Hyde Park, which, most of the time, were almost universally ignored, were daubed with politically inspired graffiti. A statue of James Cook erected in 1879 attracted the most attention. The words 'change the date' and 'no pride in genocide' were spray-painted on the plinth. A statue of Lachlan Macquarie, the colony's fifth governor, erected as recently as 2013 received similar attention. The country's political leaders responded with orchestrated anger. The political content was ignored. The perpetrators were 'vandals', they were guilty of 'a cowardly criminal act' in the testy words of Prime Minister Turnbull. But the action, he believed, was 'part of a deeply disturbing and totalitarian campaign to not just challenge our history but to deny it and obliterate it'.[8] The upsurge in activism following the mass protests in the United States renewed Australian demands for truth-telling, and statues of Cook were again provided with politically inspired graffiti.[9]

There has also been serious debate about amending or adding to the wording of historical artefacts to allow them to reflect changing attitudes and viewpoints. For the first time, many people were alerted to a most interesting amendment that had been added to a statue on Fremantle's esplanade. The Explorers' Monument was unveiled in 1913 to commemorate three frontiersmen – Frederick Panter, James Harding and William Goldwyer – who were killed by Aboriginal assailants in the far north of the colony in 1864. Plaques on the monument explained how the intrepid pioneers had been murdered in their sleep by treacherous natives. There is also a bust of the leader of the official 'search and punitive expedition', who found and carried the explorers' remains back to Fremantle. About twenty Aboriginal people were killed by the punitive party. In 1994, the International Year of Indigenous Peoples, a counter-memorial was set in the monument's base. The project brought together staff and students from Murdoch University, the Fremantle City Council and local Aboriginal people who had worked with traditional bands from the La Grange region. It explained that it had been erected 'by people who found the monument before you offensive' because it described the events 'from one perspective only, the viewpoint of the white "settlers"'. The twenty Aboriginal victims were remembered, as well as 'all other Aboriginal people who died during the invasion of their country'.[10] Writing at the time of the Uluru Statement, Bruce Scates, who had been involved with the project from the earliest days, hoped that Fremantle suggested 'the way forward'.[11]

The controversy about the statues of Cook and Macquarie was an offshoot of the ongoing contention about Australia Day and the questions raised before the impending commemoration of the 250th anniversary of Cook's voyage along the east coast in 1770. It pinned the debate down to the very early years of British colonisation, leaving the rest of the 19th century in the shadows. This recapitulated much of the historical literature, which had dealt with the early years but set the subject aside long before the conquest of northern Australia was underway. And that is where our truth-telling is most urgently required. The reasons for this have been already discussed. There were two quite distinct eras of colonisation and spoliation. The first ran from 1788 to 1856 everywhere except Western Australia, the second from the 1850s until the first half of the 20th century. Different parts of the continent were involved. But of greater significance was the fact that what happened during the first phase of colonisation was the responsibility of the British government. It was an imperial project. The major political decisions were made in London. There was little that anyone in the colonies could do to change the broad outlines of policy. Moral responsibility largely resided offshore. The story in both New South Wales and Tasmania was complicated by the convict system. The prisoners were not like the normal colonist. They were conscripts with no choice in the matter. They were thrust into roles they did not choose for themselves.

Much changed in the 1850s, when the five colonies in eastern Australia were granted internal self-government with their own bicameral parliaments. Power passed from Downing Street to the colonial capitals, and that included complete power over the First Nations. The British government was frequently pushed by the humanitarian organisations to intervene in the affairs of the new parliaments, but they did little more than express discreet official concern. With political power came culpability. So while there was no pause in the outward surge of the frontier in the second half of the 19th century, there was an exchange of moral responsibility. Truth-telling in this instance does not lead back to Britain, but to the increasingly democratic colonial parliaments. We cannot disown what was done in Australia by Australians to Australians. And in the major colonies political decisions were within the reach of the newly enfranchised electorates. Policy regarding the Aboriginal peoples might have been reformed, but by and large it wasn't. If anything things got worse. Colonial self-government did no favours for the First Nations. They would have been better off in Crown colonies ruled from Britain, as the example of Western Australia illustrates.

The imperial government handed Queensland and South Australia an extraordinary legacy. They became responsible for two-thirds of tropical Australia to do with as they wished. Much of it was virtually unknown to the Europeans apart from the accounts of a handful of explorers. But it was clear that there were large Indigenous nations with little knowledge of white settlers. All the experience that had been gained during the first two generations suggested that the frontiersmen would have to fight their way into Aboriginal homelands and then use punitive violence to maintain their position. The restraints that had been imposed by British governors could be ignored, as inadequate as they had been. Two aspects of the law were at the centre of the colonial rebellion, which succeeded by the simple process of ignoring laws that had been inherited from the imperial administrations. And they were of profound importance to what happened to the First Nations under the new regime. They were about both land and life itself.

We have already seen how the British government designed a very specific form of land tenure when it created the pastoral lease that was imposed on the Australian colonies and protected from future local amendment. It recognised the right of Aboriginal people to remain on their traditional lands, regardless of the parallel right of pastoralists to graze their animals on the same country. It had been made absolutely clear that it was illegal to force Aboriginal bands off their land. The enduring legal force of this law was affirmed by the High Court in 1996. But that had no effect at all on the expansion of settlement in the second half of the 19th century. The law was simply ignored. Governments did not enforce it. It had no influence on the behaviour of the great majority of frontiersmen. There is no known attempt by the colonial judiciary or by the whole legal profession to call the governments to account. None of the many lawyers who became leading politicians did anything about it. In 1887, the government resident in the Northern Territory reported on the ongoing violence as pastoralists moved onto Aboriginal land. He referred to and quoted from the relevant clause in the pastoral leases but remarked that they were observed 'rather in a poetic than a practical sense'.[12] He realised that it was a matter of life and death. If the law had been enforced, hundreds of lives would have been saved. As we have already seen, Earl Grey had appreciated this when the pastoral leases were created. In a memo he explained to his officers that they would protect the Aboriginal people from being exterminated.

The second profoundly contentious aspect of the law inherited from the era of imperial administration was the rule that the people of the First Nations were, without exception, British subjects. Where this really mattered was when Aboriginal people were killed. In theory their death was to be treated in the same way as the death of a white person, as murder or manslaughter, unless there were mitigating circumstances. Violent death should be followed by an investigation, an inquest and a trial. If found guilty, the perpetrator would face the full force of the law, which would, in normal circumstances, mean capital punishment. But the problem was that very few colonists accepted the basic premise of the law. They refused to accommodate the underlying assumption of racial equality: while killing blacks might be regrettable, it was often necessary and entirely excusable. It should never lead to a white man being tried, let alone executed.

The colonial governments did not publicly endorse the overwhelming public view of the matter, but their behaviour gave them away, and this was obviously the case in the colonies still engaged in promoting new settlement in Aboriginal homelands. There were very few prosecutions for killing out on the frontier. In Queensland and the Northern Territory there was no expectation that even large-scale killing would result in prosecution. On those occasions when white men were arrested on suspicion of murder, usually in a town rather than out in the bush, juries were notoriously reluctant to return a guilty verdict and almost never did.

Truth-telling allows little room to manoeuvre. The conquest of the north pursued by the self-governing colonies was decisively more brutal than what had happened in the south of the continent under imperial rule. New generations of frontiersmen rode deep into tropical Australia, schooled in both bushcraft and killing, and carrying new, more efficient weapons. There seems to be little doubt that thousands of Aboriginal people were sacrificed in the frenetic crusade to settle the north. Far fewer white men died than was the case in the south. The frontier was a long way from Brisbane, Adelaide and Perth. But the colonial politicians knew the way things were. They were enablers. They accepted that violence was necessary and a price they were willing, vicariously, to pay. Some expressed regret about the Indigenous victims but many looked the other way, believing that it was the law of nature that inferior races would pass away. The colonial newspapers frequently carried reports from the front line. The reading public was certainly aware of what was going on, and there was always a minority whose consciences would not let them rest. But their often lonely vigil reminds us of the need to give serious consideration to the careers of the leading politicians who were ultimately responsible for what happened during those years when the 'line of blood' stretched across vast areas of the north.

Australians have been ready to call the early governors – Phillip, Macquarie, Brisbane, Arthur and Stirling – to account for killing that occurred on their watch. But far less attention has been paid to the colonial leaders who were deeply implicated in the conquest of the north – men like Sir John Forrest, Sir John Downer and Sir Samuel Griffith. It is not clear why. The colonial governors were men who were educated and grew up in the 18th century. They were imperial officials who served out their term in Australia and then departed never to return. The colonial leaders are much closer to us, culturally and temporally. They were Australian by birth or adoption. They were responsible to the local electors, not to a distant bureaucracy. Each one served as premier of their colony: Forrest in Western Australia from 1890 to 1901, Downer in South Australia twice between 1885 and 1893, and Griffith

in Queensland twice between 1883 and 1893. Both Downer
and Griffith had terms as their colony's attorney-general. All
three were eminent men, knighted for their services. They
were fathers of federation. Griffith was one of the principal
drafters of the Constitution and went on to be the first Chief
Justice of the High Court, a role he served in until 1919. Both
Downer and Forrest entered the new federal parliament, and
Forrest held many senior portfolios until his death in office in
1918. They were men to be reckoned with, at the forefront of
Australian politics and jurisprudence for forty or fifty years.
Each of them had a Canberra suburb named in their honour.
Their roles in the destruction of Aboriginal society over vast
areas of the continent are rarely celebrated, commemorated or
even discussed.

Forrest bestrode the new parliament in Perth for the ten
years that also witnessed the violent suppression of Aboriginal resistance in the Kimberley. The Forrest family, including John's brother Alexander, were deeply involved in the
whole venture as leaseholders, managers and financiers. It
should come as no surprise that the new government showed
no respect for the Aboriginal rights embodied in the pastoral leases. But as a leading surveyor for many years, it is quite
improbable that Forrest didn't know about them. In his recent
study on policing of the Kimberley frontier from 1882 to 1905
entitled *'Every Mother's Son is Guilty'*, Chris Owen observed
that by the mid 1890s the police had begun systematically
eradicating Aboriginal people from pastoral land and that the
government was aware of what was happening. In July 1895,
Forrest's undersecretary Octavius Burt wrote a memo to him

stating that 'there can be no doubt that from these frequent reports that a war of extermination is being waged on these unfortunate blacks in the Kimberley district ...' Surely, he added plaintively, 'this is a thing that should not be'. Owen added that there was no indication that either Forrest or the commissioner of police took any action after reading Burt's memo.[13]

The same complicity in extreme violence is apparent in the career of John Downer, who was premier when the grasslands of the Gulf Country were thrown open for settlement. In his 2009 essay, 'The brutal truth: what happened in the Gulf Country', Tony Roberts investigated the extent to which governments in Adelaide condoned or turned a blind eye to frontier massacres in the Gulf Country up until 1910. He estimated that at least 600 men, women, children and babies, or about one-sixth of the population, were killed. No one was charged with these murders. There were twenty white deaths. There was, he observed, no regard for the legal and human rights of the Aboriginal owners of the land, no explanations, no consultations.

Having closely examined the incriminating records of the frontier period Roberts concluded that Downer's name was mentioned more frequently than any of his colleagues. He explained that there were dozens of massacres in the Gulf Country while Downer was attorney-general between 1881 and 1884 and both premier and attorney-general between 1885 and 1887. As attorney-general he ignored the Aboriginal rights embodied in every one of the pastoral leases issued for the Gulf Country. It is beyond belief that, as a leading lawyer, he didn't know the fine detail of the leases. It was a deliberate defiance of the law. Roberts appreciated that Downer could have changed the course of pastoral settlement in the Territory and saved many hundreds of lives had he upheld the law; instead, 'his illegal policy set the pattern'.[14] Downer nailed his colours to the mast when he personally defended the notorious policeman William Willshire, who was on trial for murder in July 1891. Despite his reputation for extreme brutality Downer was able to destroy the case for the prosecution, and the Port Augusta jury returned a not guilty verdict after fifteen minutes to the applause of the audience. The crowd outside the courthouse cheered when Willshire appeared.[15]

Downer may not have known that Samuel Griffith established a similar pattern of behaviour during his period as Queensland's attorney-general between 1874 and 1878. The question merits further investigation, but we can assume that many pastoral leases were issued during these years, and as far as we can tell Griffith took no action to protect Aboriginal rights to remain on and use their traditional lands. In other words he actively condoned widespread defiance of the law. The instructions issued to the native police to 'disperse' all large gatherings of Aboriginal people were obviously at odds with the letter of the law. The seriousness of this dereliction of duty has commonly been overlooked. But there is no doubt that Roberts was right. If the conditions in the leases had been enforced, the blood-soaked history of pastoral expansion may have been quite different. Earl Grey had understood in 1848 what tragic outcomes would follow if the First Nations could be driven from their country. Looking back in 1992, the High

Court justices Deane and Gaudron declared that 'the oppression and, in some areas of the continent, the obliteration or near obliteration of the Aborigines were the inevitable consequences of their being dispossessed of their traditional lands'.[16] We don't know if the two judges were aware of the prominent role played in this epic tragedy by the man who was the chief justice of their court from its foundation in 1903 until 1919.

Griffith was at the centre of Queensland politics for twenty years from 1874 until 1893, when he became the colony's chief justice. He was premier between 1883 and 1888, and again between 1890 and 1893. This was the time when the frontiersmen drove their sheep and cattle into the far corners of the colony and then on into the Northern Territory. Sugar planters and small selectors began clearing tracts of tropical rainforest. In coastal areas, young men and women were being taken up, often forcibly, into the burgeoning pearling industry. There was perpetual conflict with Aboriginal bands defending their homelands. The native police force continued to patrol the fringes of settlement. Hundreds of men, women and children were killed. Like his colonial contemporaries Forrest and Downer, Griffith knew exactly what was happening out there in the vast hinterland. He did little to stop the killing. How then should history remember him? Will his high reputation survive the rigours of truth-telling? Perhaps more to the point, should it survive?

13

INESCAPABLE ICONOCLASM

I began thinking about the reputation of Samuel Walker Griffith in 2018 while reading the *Griffith Review* no. 60, entitled *First Things First*. It was an edition that 'focused solely on Indigenous issues, written predominantly by Aboriginal and Torres Strait Islander people', and was a response to the Turnbull government's rejection of the proposals contained in the Uluru Statement. The opening page, as in all volumes of the *Griffith Review*, bore a tribute to Griffith himself. It began with the statement that he was 'one of Australia's great early achievers' and then noted the high points of his political and judicial career. It followed with the observation that he was 'an important reformer and legislator, a practical and cautious man of words'. The tribute continued:

> Griffith died in 1920 and is now best remembered in
> his namesakes: an electorate, a society, a suburb and a
> university ... His commitment to public debate and ideas,
> his delight in words and art, and his attachment to active
> citizenship are recognised by the publication that bears
> his name ... Like Sir Samuel Griffith, *Griffith Review* is

iconoclastic and non-partisan, with a sceptical eye and a pragmatically reforming heart and a commitment to public discussion.[1]

My interest was renewed late in 2019, when I was in Brisbane at the time of Griffith University's sixth Integrity Conference, which included the Griffith Lecture delivered by Judge Navi Pillay on the subject of 'The future of human rights and the rule of law'. Judge Pillay was a good choice. She had been a judge at the International Criminal Court in The Hague and High Commissioner for Human Rights at the United Nations from 2008 to 2014.

It was irresistible not to consider how appropriate Griffith's name was to be used as the banner headline for a lecture on such a subject delivered by a distinguished jurist whose life's work has been about human rights and international criminal law. Was she told anything about Griffith's career? But more immediately, I wondered if the *Review*'s proclaimed iconoclasm had ever been directed inward or its 'sceptical eye' ever turned on its eponymous patron? These are fair questions and need to be answered. *First Things First* was, after all, published in response to the Uluru Statement, which placed truth-telling near the top of its agenda.

It is necessary then to look again at Griffith's political career. During the two decades between 1874 and 1893 he was a senior minister in three administrations, once as attorney-general, twice as premier. Anyone familiar with Queensland history will be aware that these years witnessed the continuing expansion of settlement, with First Nations being thrust aside and hundreds if not thousands killed. There were hundreds of monthly patrols by the native police, a heavily armed force whose official instructions were, as we have seen, to disperse any large gatherings of Aboriginal people and to respond to complaints from settlers with punitive violence. The realities of frontier conflict were well known. No Queenslander with any interest in public affairs could be unaware of the way things were. Griffith sat in and presided over cabinet meetings during his twelve years in office. Along with his ministerial colleagues, he was not only complicit in the killing, he was personally responsible for it. That is the inescapable fact about cabinet responsibility in the system of government inherited from the British. He may have had few contacts with Aboriginal people, had rarely travelled out into the vast hinterland, and may have had little to do with native police officers, but that is all beside the point. Someone had to have been responsible for the killing, and the only place to look is at the cabinet ministers.

But why single out Griffith? That is a reasonable question. His ability in, and great grasp of the law, praised in numerous accounts of his career makes him especially culpable. Many Queenslanders, and certainly some members of parliament, probably believed that it was both morally and legally permissible to kill Aboriginal people who resisted the spread of settlement. It must have seemed that there was, in effect, a local law that allowed this to happen. That was a conclusion many people came to and declared to be the case in correspondence in the newspapers. Griffith himself appears to have had similar thoughts, and in the critical debate on the native police in parliament in 1880, said that he did not think that 'all cases of reprisals should be treated as murders' because there were many situations in which 'recourse could only be had to the tribal law, and in which it would be absurd to allow the offence to go unavenged'.[2] But there was nothing in the law in Britain or Australia that allowed murder to be disregarded, and certainly not a word about imposing tribal law, whatever that meant in Griffith's mind. And vengeance was not an idea that sat easily with legal tradition.

The critical point here is that he was a man trained and steeped in the common law, the drafter of the Queensland Criminal Code. After all the legal situation was clear. The Aboriginal peoples were, and had been since before the establishment of the colony, British subjects. If they were killed it was murder unless there were mitigating circumstances. No other interpretation was possible.

Griffith was a liberal who had strongly opposed the Pacific Island labour trade. He would have liked to replace the native police and said so in private and occasionally in public.[3] But nothing changed until he had left the parliament. And all the time the killing went on. It may seem unfair to pick Griffith out for special condemnation. But his ability, judicial understanding and, indeed eminence, means he needs to be held to a higher standard than many of his poorly educated contemporaries. During his time in office there were hundreds of extrajudicial killings. About this there can be no doubt. He was ultimately responsible and therefore guilty of what, after 1945, came to be known as crimes against humanity. Is any other conclusion possible?

But what if frontier conflict was a form of warfare, as many people argued at the time? Does that change things? Does that mean we need to apply a different standard when judging Griffith? Was he a war leader like WM Hughes in the First World War or John Curtin in the Second? Should he be judged by the laws of war? Should he be applauded for expanding the reach of the Queensland colonial government and protecting the lives of his fellow countrymen? This might be a more honest way to proceed than simply ignoring the terrible death toll involved in conquering tropical Australia. We have already seen that many people in Queensland thought they were at war with the First Nations, and saw their situation as similar to that of European contemporaries who were thrusting imperial frontiers forward in many parts of the world.

This is exactly what happened in Argentina, which, in 1875, launched a military campaign known as the Conquest of the Desert to drive the Mapuche people off their traditional lands in Patagonia to make way for European farms and towns. The leader of the campaign was the War Minister, General Julio Roca. He became a national hero. There are thirty-six statues raised in his honour, he has dozens of streets, avenues and schools named after him. For many years his face was on the 100 peso banknote. But Roca's reputation has been overtaken by aggressive historical revisionism. There has been intense debate about his reputation, and there have been many demands to take down his statues and rename landmarks that bear his name.

If we were to reconsider Griffith as a war leader, he too might be caught up in a flurry of reinterpretation. But in

19th-century Australia there was no easy way to actually declare war on the First Nations. Legally, as we have already seen, they were British subjects, and there is no evidence that anyone in authority sought to change their status. If they were killed, the presumption had to be that they had died either as a result of murder or manslaughter.

Should Griffith's reputation matter to us? Well yes, given that he helped draft the Australian Constitution and was the first chief justice of the High Court. He was at the centre of both political and judicial life during the federation's formative generation. He is far more important to us than Cook and Macquarie, whose statues have been defaced. He is more significant than John Batman, whose statue in Melbourne has been removed and whose name has been taken from an electorate in the city, or Angus McMillan, the pioneer of Gippsland whose name has similarly been recently removed from a Victorian electorate. McMillan, Batman and Macquarie were all involved in killing Aboriginal people, but nowhere on the scale of what happened during the conquest of northern Australia. Moral condemnation seems to be easier when the subjects of our ire lived a long time ago. Should anything be done about Griffith? Or should we discreetly avert our eyes from the blood on the great man's hands? The answer we come up with will be a key indicator of whether truth-telling will bring about change, whether it will lead to fundamental reassessment of reputations or merely to an accumulation of facts.

If the Australian Electoral Commission thought it appropriate to remove the names Batman and McMillan from the list of electorates because of their involvement in frontier warfare and killing of First Nations people, should the same action be taken in the case of Griffith, whose name graces a Brisbane electorate? He oversaw far more bloodshed than the two frontiersmen. But is it a case of it being much easier to take symbolic action against the foot soldiers than against the high command and knights of the realm?

What should Griffith University do? The least we should expect is that the leadership will treat the matter with appropriate seriousness. They need to look at what many prestigious universities in Britain and the United States are doing about their involvement in the slave trade and then consider what could be done here. This should include an appropriately funded research project on Griffith's role in Queensland politics and his complicity in the destruction of Aboriginal society over large areas of the colony. His legal career could be interrogated by members of the university's own School of Criminology, which is promoted as one of the most vibrant and high-performing in the world. Why not organise a mock trial to prosecute Griffith for crimes against humanity? Biographical sketches of the kind published in the *Griffith Review* need to be dropped altogether or substantially amended. If the major public lecture is to continue to bear his name, it would only be fair to the distinguished invited lecturers to be provided with a fair assessment of his legacy. This is especially pertinent because there is a contemporary of Griffith who would be more appropriate for a named lecture. My choice would be the Danish Australian journalist Carl Feilberg, whose crusade against the treatment of the Aboriginal peoples is one of the most inspiring events in Queensland history. The collection of material that appeared in *The Queens-lander* and published under the title *The Way We Civilise* was one of the most influential political pamphlets ever published in Australia. Feilberg has recently been inducted into the Australian Media Hall of Fame.

Truth-telling is a necessary way to find new perspectives on our history. Given the way the Aboriginal peoples disappeared from our national story for more than half a century, bringing them back into a new narrative will have many consequences, some of which will be vigorously opposed. But a commitment to truth should strengthen our determination to follow where the evidence leads us, even if we need to engage in the iconoclasm that was, after all, nominated as a chosen path in the mission statement of the *Griffith Review*.

Should the university change its name? It should at least be a question open for debate. But it is pre-eminently a matter for Queensland to consider. Just recently, Brisbane's major new children's hospital had a name-change. It had been called the Lady Phyllis Cilento Hospital by then Premier Campbell Newman in December 2013, before its official opening a year later. Lady Phyllis and her husband Sir Raphael had been eminent public figures in Queensland for many years. She had been one of the first women to obtain a medical degree, and was a vigorous campaigner for better health outcomes for women and children. She wrote a series of books and regular newspaper columns. Many of her views on race and sexuality are now no longer acceptable, and a petition signed by 900 staff members called for her name to be removed from the hospital. There was considerable opposition to the change, particularly from the Cilento family. And it was expected to have an overall cost of $500 000. But the health minister in the Labor government, Steven Miles, took up the cause and in December 2018 workers began removing the large signs on the exterior of the building. How inconsequential Lady Phyllis's offences against contemporary sensibilities appear, however, when compared with the men who for fifty years funded and directed a paramilitary force that was authorised to 'disperse' any large gathering of Aboriginal men, women and children.

American universities have been wrestling with the problems arising from their historical association with slavery, and this has often been connected with the names of slave owners and traders who bequeathed money to the older of the institutions. Campaigns have also been launched to expunge the names of men known to have been involved in lynching or who were leaders of the Ku Klux Klan in the late 19th and early 20th centuries. But the most consequential recent development has been the decision of Princeton University to remove the name of Woodrow Wilson from its public policy school and a residential college. Wilson had been the university president from 1902 to 1910 before becoming president of the country in 1913, when he segregated the federal public service. As the current president of the university explained, the board of trustees found that Wilson's 'racist thinking and policies make him an inappropriate namesake for a school or college whose scholars, students and alumni must stand firmly against racism in all its forms'.[4]

Other universities have decided not to engage in name-changing but to adopt other policies as a means of historical remediation. And this is a course that both Griffith University and the Queensland government could profitably pursue. A close and contemporaneous American parallel with the frontier killing in Queensland was the widespread practice of lynching, which reached its most intense phase in the 1890s. It was clearly a matter of extrajudicial killing that was widely approved in the southern states, quite regardless of the formal legal situation. As in Queensland, the law was just ignored. But it was not forgotten and has now been publicly remembered – if not exactly commemorated – in a spectacular new museum in Montgomery, Alabama.

This is what is required in Queensland – a well-funded museum that will tell the story of the frontier wars. It is the least that might be expected from a state whose wealth has been largely due to the exploitation of the territories of the First Nations. It is a project that Griffith University is ideally placed to promote, develop and partly fund. After all, it is an inescapable responsibility that comes with the name.

CONCLUSION:
THE RESURGENT NORTH

Two aspects of the Uluru Statement inspired this book. The first related to sovereignty. The document declared that the Aboriginal and Torres Strait Islander peoples were the first sovereign nations of the Australian continent and its adjacent islands, and possessed this land under their own laws and customs. An even more controversial statement followed: 'It [the sovereignty] has never been ceded or extinguished, and co-exists with the sovereignty of the Crown.'[1] Two challenging propositions advanced together. The first was that the Australian tribes were sovereign nations and possessed their homelands under their own laws and customs. For most of settler Australia's history, this would have been a contentious view, dismissed with what might be called sympathetic scorn. It pressed against generations of prejudice, fortified by the great weight of pan-European disrespect for 'savages' and 'inferior' races. Concomitant contempt was rife in the country for many years. But as we have seen, there was more support in the thinking of international jurists over several centuries for the recognition of the rights of the worlds' tribal peoples than most Australians would have thought possible.

The dramatic changes that swept the world in the second half of the 20th century as a result of decolonisation and the decisive rejection of hitherto accepted racial ideas, eventually brought about a total revaluation of small-scale traditional societies and their place in the world. The all-important land-mark was the acceptance by the UN General Assembly of the Declaration on the Rights of Indigenous Peoples in 2007. Australia ratified the document two years later. That did not mean that there had been a sea change in public opinion. And perhaps more to the point, there has been no reassessment of Australian law, which remains chained to structures that date from the late 18th century. And they are laws bequeathed to us by imperial Britain. The courts have made it clear that they are reluctant to weaken those inherited structures, which points very dramatically to the urgent national need for the negotiation of treaties to recast the relationship between the First Nations and the Australian state. The importance of this task is frequently misunderstood. It is pressed forward by generations of injustice and by a refusal to accept that the First Nations are not just another minority group to be placed among the mosaic of multicultural Australia. They are the inheritors of ancient cultures with roots that have a depth in our soil hard for non-Indigenous Australians to comprehend. The Statement from the Heart explained that the men and women coming from 'all points of the southern sky' believed their ancient sovereignty could 'shine through as a fuller expression of Australia's nationhood'.

It could be seen as a challenge. But it was much more than that. It was by any fair measure the most significant gesture of accommodation and reconciliation ever made to settler Aus-tralia in 230 years. Treaties would also recast our relationship with Britain, allowing us to shift the burden inherited from the profoundly flawed plans made for the original settlement. We could finally slough off the deadly incubus of *terra nullius*. The High Court made a start with the *Mabo* judgment in 1992. Treaties would allow us to complete the liberation. They would also represent a major milestone in Australia's slow, sluggish progression towards completed decolonisation.

Whenever the Statement from the Heart is discussed it will always be linked with its peremptory rejection by Prime Minister Malcolm Turnbull. It was unexpected. But it was more than that, much more. It was profoundly disrespectful to all those men and women who had come together 'from all parts of the southern sky'. And to all the communities they represented. How does one explain such a stinging, collective insult? We have to assume that it was a considered reaction and that not only did Turnbull feel he had nothing to lose as a consequence but that he would win approval from many of the colleagues who sat behind him in the parliament. He may not have appreciated, however, that the brutal rebuff evoked deep historical resonance. As we have seen, Australian history is replete with the innumerable ways the First Nations have been treated with radical disrespect. It began before the first settlers arrived and has continued in one way or another ever since. This is one aspect of our history still awaiting strenuous truth-telling.

Terra nullius arrived with the First Fleet, its plans premised on the assumption that the Aboriginal inhabitants were uniquely primitive and lacking in laws and government, wandering without design over the terrain. The legal instruments designed to meet these circumstances are still with us. When conflict broke out, it rapidly became accepted in colonial society that because Aboriginal people were, in their opinion, more animal than human, killing them did not bring the legal consequences, the moral opprobrium or the burden of sin that followed the murder of a fellow white man. And that attitude was carried with the frontiersmen into every corner of the continent and was still being expressed in the memory of people alive today. Under the shadow of unpunished and unrebuked killing, lesser violence flourished. Bashing, kicking, flogging and raping Aboriginal servants, neighbours and even strangers passed without wonder in many places well into the 20th century. European ethnography at the time of the earliest settlements consigned the Aboriginal peoples to the lowest level of what was known as the Great Chain of Being. They were the most primitive Stone Age people in the world. And then, in the second half of the 19th century, when evolution captured the mind and the imagination of Europeans, Aboriginal people were seen as one of the inferior races destined to be swept away by the iron laws of the new science. It was common to hear Australians declaring that the Aboriginal people were dying out right up until the 1940s. But when the population stabilised and actually began increasing, assimilationist policies were implemented to 'breed out the colour'. All these views were shared by the community at large and significant numbers of leading intellectuals and scientists. It was this inherited disrespect that allowed prominent historians to totally neglect the First Nations up until the 1960s and to dismiss them as being no more than a melancholy anthropological footnote. At the same time, leading jurists were legitimising *terra nullius* by explaining that the Aboriginal peoples were no more than a wandering, disorganised rabble. As with so many of the disasters that ravaged the Aboriginal community, their terrible fate was attributed to their own deficiencies. We should never forget that it took the Australian judiciary 204 years to remedy the grievous fault in our land law that had been sacrosanct since 1788.

These are all lessons that have to be reinforced with sharply focused truth-telling. And they should never be forgotten. Our First Nations have been treated with such profound disrespect that it runs like a dark and ugly thread throughout the history of settler Australia. So whether he realised it or not, Malcolm Turnbull's rejection of the Statement from the Heart put him at the head of a long draft of scornful countrymen that reaches far back into our colonial past. But like many of his legal predecessors, Turnbull showed little interest in the ongoing problems in Australian jurisprudence that have already been discussed above.

Truth-telling is the ultimate gesture of respect. It indicates a willingness to listen, to learn and to concede that the stories should be heard of those who have been victims of great wrongs. That is the single most important lesson from all of the world's many truth commissions. Regardless of the long-term results, and they varied widely, victims of human rights abuses found it empowering to be able to tell their stories in a public forum. Many of the commissions were about recent events, but some of the search for answers did delve into historical injustice. This is relevant to the Australian experience. Trauma can leave behind intergenerational scars and inherited disadvantage that can only be understood historically. Groups that have suffered in the past need to understand the provenance of their present predicament. So frontier violence remains a subject of intense interest, as we have already seen. One side of the debate derides the 'black-armband' historians, and frets about the nation's self-respect and older, more benign albeit faltering narratives. The opposing side demands clear-eyed accounting, talks about 'white blindfolds' and reminds the nation of its all but sacred phrase 'Lest We Forget'.

The research of the last twenty years has put the reality of frontier violence beyond reasonable doubt. But many related problems still require answers. One of the most intriguing ones is why did the country's leading post-war historians not notice it at all? Was it oversight or deliberate evasion? How could they think that Australians had been slow to kill one another, that frontiersmen rarely had to go armed into the outback and that we had an inimitably peaceful history? But just think for one moment that the bodies had been white, that tens of thousands of our ancestors had been killed in Australia as a result of a long-running civil war. It would have become one of the most studied, most commemorated subjects in our history. There would be shelves of books about it in our libraries and bookshops. There would be relevant monuments all over the country.

A theme closely related to the idea of peaceful settlement is the belief that the Aboriginal peoples were unable or unwilling to fight for their country and way of life. They lacked the spirit and the morale of other more militant people, like Native Americans, Māori or the Bantu. That was why they simply didn't matter in our history. It is as if they hadn't earned our respect or even our interest. If they weren't written about it was their own fault. They deserved their demotion to a melancholy anthropological footnote. This profound lack of respect emerged again during the history wars, which began after the accession of Prime Minister John Howard in 1996. The fiercest critics of 'black-armband' history conceded that there was violence on the frontier, albeit exaggerated for political reasons, but claimed that the Aboriginal peoples were principally interested in plunder and had no higher motive whatsoever. They were criminals rather than warriors and patriots, and what is more, because they had no commitment to country, their violence lacked any extenuating features at all. What we should still find disturbing about this interpretation is that it found many adherents, some in the most influential positions in the land. Its leading proponent received the patronage of Prime Minister Howard.

Frontier violence has been a recurring theme of this book. It should alert us to the fact that it was endlessly discussed by our ancestors and that they argued about questions that are still pertinent and as relevant today as they were almost 200 years ago. They have not gone away. It was generally conceded that some conflict was inevitable. It accompanied European colonists wherever they went. Few people shrank from that assessment. But was it needlessly, even inexcusably violent? That was a challenging question then and still is. There is no doubt that the decision by the British to abandon the tradition of treaty-making was a portentous and tragic one that condemned a great many men, women and children to violent deaths. Treaties would have meant that the First Nations would have eventually lost control of much of their land, but far fewer would have been killed as a consequence. It is likely that many of the small First Nations that were almost completely destroyed would have survived, along with their distinct languages, history and traditions. So the British propelled the colonies along violent paths, but having done so they did attempt to manage a situation, which, they realised, had become completely out of their control once the squatters rode off into the vast hinterland. The men in the Colonial Office expressed far greater anguish about the violence than the colonists. As is well known, in 1838 the New South Wales government, under the British governor George Gipps, twice tried and then hanged seven stockmen involved in the Myall Creek massacre. It was a very different story once power passed to colonial parliaments and the frontiersmen advanced into the tropical north. Sir John Downer's personal defence of the violent South Australian policeman William Willshire was as significant and symbolic an event as the Myall Creek trial half a century earlier.

Another question that has haunted Australia for a long time is whether frontier conflict was a kind of warfare. It matters a great deal if the answer is yes. It means that we have two quite distinct kinds of war. One relates, almost without exception, to the Australian engagement in imperial wars, mainly situated a long way away; the other to the more enduring conflict fought in Australia about sovereignty and the control of land.

This is an unusual situation. In comparable countries, conflict with the First Nations is accepted as part of the larger story of warfare. The United States list of official wars, for instance, includes even the smallest, little-known Indian Wars, alongside the War of Independence, the Civil War and the great conflicts of the 20th century. As we have already seen, this presents us with the problem of how our own domestic war should be commemorated. We remember our overseas wars with deep and continuing reverence. We invest large amounts of public money in the project of commemoration. Our young people are encouraged to view the men and women who didn't return with wide-eyed admiration. The landing at Gallipoli is presented to them as the true birth of the nation. So how are we to find a place for the men and women of the First Nations who died fighting for country, kin and customs? When will Australia find appropriate ways to illustrate that it recognises, values and respects their sacrifice?

Northern Australia has featured in this book. That focus reflects the fact that I spent most of my professional career in North Queensland. In teaching Australian history in that environment one necessary task was to remedy the almost complete neglect of the tropical north in the major history texts of the time. Otherwise local students would come away with the idea that nothing of importance had ever happened in their part of Australia. But it is obvious now that the two central themes of First Nation's sovereignty and truth-telling have to be tracked deep into the tropics, north of Capricorn. Aboriginal resistance there was widespread, the violence of the frontiersmen was unrestrained, unrebuked and unpunished.

Men out on the frontier in the late 19th century had inherited a tradition of violence, an emerging confidence in the bush and highly efficient firearms. They had become symbolic of the new nation which admired their toughness and resourcefulness. And as we have seen their brutality received no sanction from the new generation of colonial leaders who shepherded their people into the new federal government on the first day of the new century the blood on their hands notwithstanding.

But the most striking aspect of the colonial thrust into northern Australia was that it faltered. The frontiersmen were indeed formidable but there were never enough of them. The leaders of the new nation looked north with evident anxiety. There were far more Aborigines, Islanders and Asian sojourners than white people. There was a growing population of mixed-descent children which evoked unease about racial degeneration. But it was assumed that white women and children would not flourish in the tropics. There were still in 1901 large areas of the north where few Europeans had ever been and where Indigenous traditions persisted undisturbed. This presented the highly challenging question about sovereignty. Was it all in the hands of the federal parliament meeting far away in Melbourne and men who, almost without exception, had never been in the north and never would be? It appeared to be an easy matter to assume that they were inheritors of British claims of sovereignty made in 1788, 1824 and 1829. It seemed neat and decisive and came with the authority and prestige of the British Crown still represented by a failing Queen Victoria when the federation was proclaimed.

But things looked very different when viewed from the north. While it seemed a simple matter to describe how the new Commonwealth had acquired sovereignty, it was far more problematic to explain how the First Nations had lost it. And not just how but when. There is still no convincing explanation. The Australian courts have declared that they are unable to question the Crown's capacity to exercise prerogative powers. It should come as no surprise to discover that Aboriginal and Torres Strait Islander people living in their homelands are convinced that they still exercise a form of sovereignty within the boundaries of their traditional territories. That seems a more plausible explanation of the situation on the ground than what is provided by conventional legal doctrine. And so it was that delegates from 'all points of the southern sky' who attended the Constitutional Convention at Uluru in May 2017 declared that their sovereignty had 'never been ceded or extinguished, and co-exists with the sovereignty of the Crown'. It was much more than a rhetorical flourish. It was a declaration of high seriousness and, as we have seen, has the weight of history behind it. Their critical question 'How could it be otherwise?' is a profound challenge to white Australia. It sits there unanswered in the inboxes of the nation's leaders in both our parliaments and our courts.

Such a challenge could be ignored in 1901 and for much of the 20th century. But things are different now – very different. Northern Australia has experienced a set of profound changes, which viewed together represent what is in effect a counter-revolution. In 1901 and for years after, the dominant view was that the First Nations would gradually dwindle away. They had no future. But since the Second World War there has been a demographic resurgence. Meanwhile, the successful campaigns for land rights have seen up to 2 500 000 square kilometres or 32 per cent of the continental land mass returned to traditional owners.[2] It amounts to 93 per cent of the Kimberley.[3] A second and related transformation has been the return of traditional owners to their own particular clan territories to establish small outstations. The movement began in earnest in the 1970s. There are now over 1000 outstations occupied permanently or on a part-time basis. There are about 630 in the Northern Territory.[4] The First Nations are back in occupation of their territories. This represents a change with dramatic consequences. It gives the First Nations control over lands and waterways of environmental importance. But they are also of even greater strategic significance – places like the Tiwi Islands and the Torres Strait Islands, and thousands of kilometres of vulnerable northern coastline.

The founders of the federation hoped that white men would eventually people the tropical north. They failed to do so. Governments still commission reports about how to facilitate northern development. The irony is that the great national project has been brought to fruition by the men and women of the First Nations. They have repeopled the north. While not having that specific intention, they have created a situation whereby the Australian state can at last establish the fact that it is now in effective occupation of the north, largely by people who have a double claim on the land, firstly as Australian citizens and then as Indigenous people whose rights are based on international law and custom. The second may be more persuasive in the long run than the first in the world beyond Australia's borders. The time may come when the Australian state needs the First Nations as much as they need the state. The other possibility is that the First Nations will become alienated from the domestic political system and increasingly look overseas in their search for both justice and respect.

NOTES

Abbreviations

AGPS	Australian Government Publishing Service
AJCP	Australian Joint Copying Project
ALJR	*Australian Law Journal Reports*
ALR	*Australian Law Reports*
AOT	Archives Office of Tasmania
BPP	*British Parliamentary Papers*
CLR	*Commonwealth Law Reports*
CO	Colonial Office
CPD	*Commonwealth Parliamentary Debates*
CRS	Commonwealth Record Series
CSO	Colonial Secretary's Office
CUP	Cambridge University Press
DLR	*Dominion Law Review*
FLR	*Federal Law Reports*
GPO	Government Publishing Office (US)
HRA	*Historical Records of Australia*
HRNSW	*Historical Records of New South Wales*
JCU	James Cook University
ML	Mitchell Library, State Library of New South Wales
MUP	Melbourne University Press
NAA	National Archives of Australia
NSWLR	*New South Wales Law Reports*
OUP	Oxford University Press
QPD	*Queensland Parliamentary Debates*
SAPP	*South Australian Parliamentary Papers*
SLV	State Library of Victoria
SSRN	Social Science Research Network
THRA	Tasmanian Historical Research Association
UQP	University of Queensland Press
UWAP	UWA (University of Western Australia) Publishing

The Uluru Statement from the Heart

1   'The Uluru Statement from the Heart', Uluru Statement, ulurustatement.org/
     the-statement. Original italics.

Introduction: Hearing the Statement from the Heart

1   Cited by M Grattan (ed.), *Reconciliation*, Bookman Press, Melbourne, 2000,
     p. 61.
2   'The Uluru Statement from the Heart', ulurustatement.org/the-statement.
3   WEH Stanner, *After the Dreaming*, ABC, Sydney, 1968, p. 25.

1   Taking possession

1   H Grotius, *The Right of War and Peace*, 2 vols, London, 1738, vol. 2, p. 550.
2   AG Price, *The Explorations of Captain James Cook*, Angus & Robertson, Sydney,
     1958, p. 19.
3   JC Beaglehole (ed.), *The Journals of Captain Cook on his Voyages of Discovery*,
     2 vols, CUP, Cambridge, 1955–74, vol. 1, p. 514.
4   Quoted in MF Lindley, *The Acquisition and Government of Backward Territory
     in International Law*, Longmans, Green & Co., London, 1926, p. 29.
5   J Story, *Commentaries on the Constitution of the United States*, 5th edn,
     M Bigelow (ed.), Little, Brown & Co., Boston, 1891, p. 6.
6   Lindley, *The Acquisition and Government of Backward Territory*, pp. 26–27.
7   H Grotius, *The Freedom of the Seas, or, the Right Which Belongs to the Dutch to
     Take Part in the East Indian Trade*, (1605), trans. R Van Deman Magoffin, OUP,
     New York, 1916, p. 12.
8   JG Heineccius, *A Methodical System of Universal Law, or, the Laws of Nature and
     Nations Deduced from Certain Principles, and Applied to Proper Cases*,
     2 vols, trans. G Turnbull, J Noon, London, 1741, vol. 1, p. 182.
9   J Cook, *The Voyage of the* Resolution *and* Discovery, JC Beaglehole (ed.), CUP,
     Cambridge, 1967, p. ccxxiii.
10   Committee on Transportation, 28 July 1785, *Journals of the House of Commons*,
     vol. 40, 1803, p. 1164.
11   T Twiss, *The Oregon Question Examined, in Respect to Facts and the Law of
     Nations*, Longman, Brown, Green, and Longmans, New York, 1846, p. 19;
     J Simsarian, 'The acquisition of legal title to terra nullius', *Political Science
     Quarterly*, vol. 53, no. 1, 1938, p. 121.
12   'James Maria Matra's proposal', *HRNSW*, vol. 1, part 2, p. 1.
13   J Banks, *The* Endeavour *Journal*, 2 vols, JC Beaglehole (ed.), Angus &
     Robertson, Sydney, 1962, vol. 2, pp. 230–32.
14   Anon., *Copious Remarks on the Discovery of New South Wales*, printed for the
     booksellers in town and country, London, 1787, p. 51; Anon., *The History of
     New Holland*, John Stockdale, London, 1787, p. 232.
15   Quoted in RJ King, 'Terra Australis: terra nullius aut terra aboriginum?',
     Journal of the Royal Australian Historical Society, vol. 72, no. 4, October 1986,
     p. 77.
16   Phillip to Nepean, 9 July 1788, and Phillip to Sydney, 10 July 1788, *HRA*,
     series 1, no. 1, pp. 56, 62.
17   W Tench, *Sydney's First Four Years*, (1788), Angus & Robertson, Sydney, 1961,
     pp. 9, 35.

18 J Hunter, *An Historical Journal of the Transactions at Port Jackson and Norfolk Island*, John Stockdale, London, 1793, p. 79.

19 Anon., *An Authentic and Interesting Narrative of the late Expedition to Botany Bay*, A Keith, Aberdeen, 1789, p. 35.

20 Phillip to Sydney, 15 May 1788, *HRA*, series 1, no. 1, pp. 30–31.

21 Phillip to Sydney, 15 May 1788.

22 Phillip to Nepean, 9 July 1788, *HRA*, series 1, no. 1, p. 58.

23 Tench, *Sydney's First Four Years*, p. 70.

24 F Barrallier, 'Journal of the expedition, undertaken by order of His Excellency Governor King, into the interior of New South Wales', 1802, trans. FM Bladen, *HRNSW*, vol. 5, p. 749.

25 K Roberts-Wray, *Commonwealth and Colonial Law*, Stevens & Sons, London, 1966, p. 631.

26 WE Hall, *A Treatise on International Law*, 8th edn, OUP, Oxford, 1924, pp. 129–30.

27 Messrs Shepherd and Gifford to Earl Bathurst, *HRA*, series 4, no. 1, p. 330.

28 *South Australia Act 1834*, 4 & 5 Wm. IV, c. 95.

29 *Wilson v Terry 1849* in JG Legge, *A Selection of Supreme Court Cases in New South Wales from 1825 to 1862*, Charles Potter, Sydney, 1896, p. 508.

30 *Cooper v Stuart* (1889) 14 App Cas 286, at p 291.

31 In *Coe v Commonwealth* (1979) 53 *ALJR* 403, Justice Lionel Murphy stated: 'Independent tribes, travelling over a territory or stopping in certain places, may exercise a de facto authority which prevents the territory being "terra nullius". Although the Privy Council referred ... to peaceful annexation ... The statement ... may be regarded ... as a convenient falsehood to justify the taking of aborigines' land.'

2 This ancient sovereignty

1 Hunter, *An Historical Journal*, pp. 47–48.

2 Tench, *Sydney's First Four Years*, p. 226.

3 See, for instance, the journal of Francis Barrallier in *HRNSW*, vol. 5, p. 771.

4 EJ Eyre, *Journals of Expeditions of Discovery into Central Australia, and Overland*, 2 vols, T and W Boone, London, 1845, vol. 1, p. 351.

5 F Tuckfield, Journal, SLV, MS 11341, p. 174.

6 Eyre, *Journals of Expeditions of Discovery*, vol. 2, p. 247.

7 G Grey, *Journals of Two Voyages of Discovery in North-West and Western Australia*, 2 vols, T and W Boone, London, 1841, vol. 2, p. 263.

8 J Grant, *The Narrative of a Voyage of Discovery*, T Egerton, London, 1803, p. 127.

9 Hunter, *Journals of Expeditions of Discovery*, p. 43.

10 L de Freycinet, *Reflections on New South Wales, 1788–1839*, (1844), trans. T Cullity, Hordern House, Sydney, 2001, p. 105.

11 W Darling to Arthur, 4 April 1832, Sir George Arthur Papers, ML, ZA 2188.

12 NJB Plomley (ed.), *Friendly Mission*, THRA, Hobart, 1966, pp. 88, 202.

13   'Zeno', *Hobart Town Gazette*, 24 July 1824.

14   *The Tasmanian*, 21 December 1827.

15   Colonial Secretary's Files, General Correspondence, CSO 1/1/323, AOT.

16   'Phillip's view on the conduct of the expedition and the treatment of convicts',
      28 February 1787, *HRNSW*, vol. 1, part 2, p. 52.

17   Governor Phillip to Lord Sydney, 26 April 1788, *HRNSW*, vol. 1, part 2, p. 128.

18   'Phillip's instructions', 25 April 1787, *HRNSW*, vol. 1, part 2, p. 89.

19   W Bradley, *A Voyage to New South Wales, 1786–92*, Ure Smith, Sydney, 1969,
      p. 59.

20   D Collins, *An Account of the English Colony in New South Wales*, T Cadell jun.
      and W Davies, London, 1798, p. 147.

21   Tench, *Sydney's First Four Years*, p. 138.

22   Tench, *Sydney's First Four Years*, p. 137.

23   Tench, *Sydney's First Four Years*, p. 208.

24   J Hunter, *An Historical Journal of Events at Sydney and at Sea, 1787–1792*, Angus
      & Robertson, Sydney, pp. 326–38.

25   Collins, *An Account of the English Colony in New South Wales*, p. 416.

26   King to Portland, 2 January 1800, *HRA*, series 1, vol. 2, p. 402.

27   L Macquarie, 'Government and General Orders', 16 December 1815; and
      'Proclamation', 8 June 1816, *HRA*, series 1, vol. 9, pp. 54, 142.

28   Bathurst to R Darling, 14 July 1825, *HRA*, series 1, vol. 12, p. 21.

29   Arthur to Stephen, Governor's Office, Despatches received by the Colonial
      Office, 3 February 1830, GO 33/7, AOT, p. 901.

30   *Military operations lately carried on against the Aboriginal inhabitants of Van
      Diemen's Land*, House of Commons Sessional Paper No. 259, 23 September
      1831, vol. 19, p. 175.

31   Stephen to Glenelg, 10 December 1835, Colonial Office, 13/3.

32   *HRA*, series 4, no. 1, p. 414.

33   *South Australia Act 1834*, 4 & 5 Wm., IV, c. 95.

34   'Proceedings of the Council, Tuesday, September 15', *South Australian Register*,
      19 September 1840. Original italics.

35   'Criminal sessions before His Honour Justice Cooper', *Adelaide Chronicle*,
      4 November 1840.

36   Arthur to Colonial Office, 24 September 1832, Colonial Office: Tasmania,
      Original Correspondence, CO 280/35, UK National Archives.

37   Published in 'Report of the Select Committee on Aborigines (British
      Settlements)', *BPP*, vol. 7, no. 425, 1837, p. 126.

38   FC Irwin, *The State and Position of Western Australia*, Simpkin, Marshall & Co.,
      London, 1835, p. 28.

3   Whose land?

1   *Milirrpum v Nabalco Pty Ltd* (1971) 17 *FLR* 141.

2   *Williams v The Attorney-General of NSW* (1913), 16 *CLR* 404, at 439. Original
      italics.

3   DP O'Connell, *International Law*, 2nd edn, 2 vols, Stevens, London, 1970, vol. 1, p. 409.

4   JR Andrews, 'The concept of statehood and the acquisition of territory in the nineteenth century', *Law Quarterly Review*, vol. 94, 1978, p. 415.

5   E Evatt, 'The Acquisition of Territory in Australia and New Zealand', *Grotian Society Papers 1968: Studies in the History of the Law of Nations*, CH Alexandrowicz (ed.), Martinus Nijhoff, The Hague, 1970, pp. 18–19.

6   J Crawford, *The Creation of States in International Law*, Clarendon Press, Oxford, 1979, p. 180.

7   E de Vattel, *The Law of Nations*, (1758), trans. CG Fenwick, Carnegie Institution, Washington DC, 1916, p. 309.

8   *US v Percheman* (1833), 32 US 51. See also H Wheaton, *Elements of International Law*, (1836), Clarendon Press, Oxford, 1936, p. 346.

9   B Pascoe, *Dark Emu*, Magabala Books, Broome, 2014.

10   Philip Gidley King Papers, series 2, ML, SAFE/C 189.

11   G Walker, letter, 29 November 1821, Bonwick Transcripts, ML, series 1, box 52.

12   Arthur to Goderich, 7 January 1832, Aboriginal Tribes in British Possessions, *BPP*, vol. 44, no. 617, 1834, p. 163.

13   GF von Martens, *The Law of Nations*, (1788), 4th edn, trans. W Cobbett, London, 1829, p. 64.

14   FC von Savigny, *Treatise on Possession*, 6th edn, trans. E Perry, S Sweet, London, 1848, pp. 5, 149, 272.

15   CF Wolff, *The Law of Nations*, (1750), 2 vols, trans. JH Drake, Clarendon Press, Oxford, 1934, vol. 2, p. 158.

16   Quoted in B Slattery, *Ancestral Lands: Alien Laws*, University of Saskatchewan, Saskatoon, 1983, p. 6.

17   *Calder v Attorney-General of British Columbia* (1973) 34 *DLR* (3d) 145, at p. 203.

18   'Instructions for our trusty and well-beloved Arthur Phillip', *HRA*, series 1, vol. 1, p. 13.

19   1787 Northwest Ordinance, quoted in HS Commager, *Documents of American History*, 6th edn, New York, 1951, pp. 128–31.

20   *Worcester v Georgia* (1832), 31 US 515 (6 Peters), at pp. 517, 543.

21   *Johnson v McIntosh* (1823), 31 US 543 (8 Wheaton), at pp. 574, 603.

22   *Mitchel v US* (1835) 34 US 711 (9 Peters), at p. 746.

23   'Papers relative to the affairs of New Zealand', *BPP*, vol. 8, no. 293, 1847, pp. 66, 64.

24   C Buxton (ed.), *Memoirs of Sir Thomas Fowell Buxton*, John Murray, London, 1848, p. 359.

25   Reports of the Select Committee on Aborigines (British Settlements), *BPP*, vol. 7, no. 538, 1836, p. 203; 1837, vol. 7, no. 425.

26   Letters Patent, Colonial Office: South Australia, Original Correspondence, CO 13/3, UK National Archives.

27   Letters from the South Australian Commission, 6 January 1836, Colonial Office, CO 386/137, UK National Archives.

28 Torrens to Glenelg, 26 December 1835, Colonial Office, CO 13/3, UK National Archives.

29 Torrens to Glenelg, 26 December 1835.

30 R Torrens, *Statement of the Origin and Progress of the Colony of South Australia*, T Brettell, London, 1849, p. 70.

31 RW Newland to Anti-Slavery Society, 8 December 1840, MSS British Empire, s. 22, Rhodes House Archive, Oxford.

32 George Augustus Robinson Journal, 1839–40, ML, A 7035, vol. 14.

33 Robinson Report for 1846, enclosed in dispatch, Fitzroy to Grey, 17 May 1847, Colonial Office, CO 201/382, UK National Archives.

34 Robinson Report for 1846.

35 Grey to Fitzroy, 11 February 1848, Colonial Office, CO 201/382, UK National Archives.

36 Grey to Fitzroy, 10 February 1850, Colonial Office, CO 208/5, UK National Archives.

37 Grey to Fitzroy, 10 February 1850.

4   Effective control?

1   Glenelg to Bourke, 26 July 1837, *HRA*, series 1, vol. 19, pp. 48–49.

2   New South Wales Government Gazette, 21 May 1839.

3   Memo on Gipps to Glenelg, 22 July 1839, Colonial Office, CO 201/286, UK National Archives.

4   Memo on Gipps to Russel, 9 April 1841, Colonial Office, CO 201/309, UK National Archives.

5   R Evans, *A History of Queensland*, CUP, Melbourne, 2007, p. 82.

6   R Fitzgerald, *From the Dreaming to 1915: A History of Queensland*, UQP, Brisbane, 1982, p. 133.

7   WK Hancock, *Australia*, Benn, London, 1930, p. 11.

8   Quoted in R Garran, *The Coming Commonwealth: An Australian Handbook of Federal Government*, Angus & Robertson, Sydney, 1897, p. 7.

9   *CPD*, vol. 4, 12 September 1901, pp. 4806–807.

10   Lindley, *The Acquisition and Government of Backward Territory*, p. 271.

11   FD Lugard, *The Dual Mandate in British Tropical Africa*, (1922), Cass, London, 1965, p. 13.

12   Lindley, *The Acquisition and Government of Backward Territory*, p. 213.

13   H Elliot, *Commonwealth Shipping Committee Report*, vol. 7, Parliamentary Sessional Papers, HM Stationery Office, London, 1881, p. 89.

14   JB Moore (ed.), *History and Digest of International Arbitrations*, GPO, Washington DC, vol. 5, 1898, pp. 4954–66.

15   Lindley, *The Acquisition and Government of Backward Territory*, p. 367.

16   'Government Resident's report for the Northern Territory', *SAPP*, vol. 2, no. 45, 1898, p. 3. Original italics.

17   'Northern Territory memorandum', 7 September 1905, *CPD*, vol. 2, no. 37, p. 14.

18 Carrodus, letter, 8 March 1940, CRS F3, Item 20/32, NAA.

19 RW Cilento & CL Lack, *Triumph in the Tropics*, Smith & Patterson, Brisbane, 1959.

20 Letter from an Elder to H Reynolds, 6 June 2000.

5 Australia and the law of nations

1 Lindley, *The Acquisition and Government of Backward Territory*, pp. 11, 20.

2 S Rachel, *Dissertations on the Law of Nature and of Nations* (1687), 2 vols, trans. JP Bate, Carnegie Institution of Washington, Washington DC, 1916, vol. 2, p. 157. Bracketed words in Ancient Greek in original.

3 Heineccius, *A Methodical System of Universal Law*, vol. 1, p. 169.

4 de Vattel, *The Law of Nations*, vol. 3, p. 11. Original italics.

5 H Wheaton, *Elements of International Law*, (1836), Oceana, New York, 1964, p. 32.

6 S von Pufendorf, *Elements of Universal Jurisprudence*, (1660), trans. WA Oldfather, Clarendon, Oxford, 1931, p. 237.

7 de Vattel, *The Law of Nations*, vol. 3, pp. 3–4.

8 C Wolff, *The Law of Nations*, p. 15.

9 J Austin, *Lectures on Jurisprudence*, 4th edn, 2 vols, John Murray, London, 1873, vol. 1, p. 233. Original italics.

10 F de Vitoria, *De Indis et de Jure Belli Relectiones*, (1532), trans. JP Bate, Carnegie, Washington DC, 1917, pp. 128–29.

11 Grotius, *The Freedom of the Seas*, (1609), trans. R Van Deman Magoffin, OUP, New York, 1916, pp. 13, 19.

12 Wolff, *The Law of Nations*, vol. 2, p. 89.

13 Wheaton, *Elements of International Law*, p. 39.

14 de Vattel, *The Law of Nations*, vol. 3, p. 11.

15 Wheaton, *Elements of International Law*, p. 18.

16 J Bentham, *A Fragment of Government*, (1776), Oxford, Clarendon Press, 1891, p. 141. Original italics.

17 W Blackstone, *Commentaries on the Laws of England*, 2 vols, 18th edn, Clarendon Press, London, 1823, pp. 26–27.

18 Austin, *Lectures on Jurisprudence*, pp. 82–89.

19 Tench, *Sydney's First Four Years*, p. 285.

20 P. de Strzelecki, *Physical Description of New South Wales and Van Diemen's Land*, Longman, Brown, Green, and Longmans, London, 1845, p. 340.

21 Eyre, *Journals of Expeditions of Discovery*, vol. 2, p. 384.

22 G Grey, *Journals of Two Expeditions of Discovery in North-West and Western Australia*, 2 vols, T and W Boone, London, 1841, vol. 2, pp. 217, 220, 223.

23 Wheaton, *Elements of International Law*, p. 18.

24 E Parker, *The Aborigines of Australia*, Hugh McColl, Melbourne, 1854, p. 12.

25 J Dredge, *Brief Notices of the Aborigines of New South Wales*, James Harrison, Geelong, 1845, pp. 6–7.

26 R O' Connor, 'Suggestions relating to the capture of the natives', Colonial Secretary's Files, CSO 1/323, AOT, p. 66.

27 EM Curr, *The Australian Race*, 4 vols, Melbourne, 1886–87, vol. 1, p. 69.

28 *Cooper v Stuart* (1989) 14 App Cas 286.

29 NSW Supreme Court Papers, 5/1161, NSW State Archives, p. 234.

30 *R v Murrell* (1836) 1 Legge 72, at p. 73.

31 NSW, Supreme Court Papers, 5/1161, NSW State Archives, p. 210.

32 NSW Supreme Court Papers, 5/1161, NSW State Archives, p. 211.

33 *R v Wedge* [1976] 1 *NSWLR* 587.

34 M Shaw, *Title to Territory in Africa: International Legal Issues*, Clarendon Press, Oxford, 1986, pp. 36–37.

35 *Coe v Commonwealth* (1979) 53 *ALJR* 403.

36 *Mabo v Queensland (No. 2)* (1992) 107 *ALR* 1, at p. 79.

37 *Mabo v Queensland (No. 2)*, at p. 121.

38 *Seas and Submerged Lands Case* (1975) 50 *ALJR* 218.

39 *Mabo v Queensland (No. 2)*, at p. 63.

40 *Mabo v Queensland (No. 2)*, at p. 30.

6   'Treaty yeh, treaty now'

1 'UN Declaration on the Rights of Indigenous Peoples', Australian Human Rights Commission, humanrights.gov.au/our-work/un-declaration-rights-indigenous-peoples-1.

2 *R v Sioui* (1990) 70 *DLR* (4th) 427, at p. 428.

3 HA Dempsey, *Crowfoot: Chief of the Blackfeet*, University of Oklahoma Press, Norman, 1972, p. 103.

4 Arthur to Goderich, 6 April 1833, Colonial Office: Tasmania, Original Correspondence, CO 280/41, UK National Archives.

7   The truth about 26 January

1 'We hereby make protest: the 1938 Day of Mourning', AIATSIS, aiatsis.gov.au/exhibitions/day-mourning-26th-january-1938.

2 'Australia Day: survey shows a majority aren't sure what it commemorates', *The Age*, 2 March 2017, www.smh.com.au/national/australia-day-survey-shows-a-majority-arent-sure-what-it-commemorates-20170301-gunnu4.html.

3 Tench, *Sydney's First Four Years*, pp. 41–42.

4 'Instructions for our trusty and well-beloved Arthur Phillip', *HRA*, series 1, vol. 1, p. 13.

5 Tench, *Sydney's First Four Years*, p. 40.

6 J Bentham, 'A plea for a constitution', *HRA*, series 4, vol. 1, p. 887.

7 *Mabo v Queensland (No. 2)* (1992) 107 *ALR* 1, at p. 55.

8 J Locke, *Two Treatises of Civil Government*, (1690), JM Dent, London, 1955, pp. 118, 180, 187.

9 H Broom, *Constitutional Law Viewed in Relation to Common Law*, 2 vols, W Maxwell, London, 1885, vol. 1, p. 225.

10   Quoted in Broom, *Constitutional Law Viewed in Relation to Common Law*, p. 231.

11   E Campbell, 'Prerogative rule in New South Wales, 1788–1823', *Journal of the Royal Australian Historical Society*, vol. 50, 1964, pp. 161–90.

12   L Fison & AW Howitt, *Kamilaroi and Kurnai*, (1880), Anthropological Publications, Oosterhout, 1967, p. 182.

13   Locke, *Two Treatises of Civil Government*, pp. 206–207.

14   Fison & Howitt, *Kamilaroi and Kurnai*, p. 182.

15   Quoted in A Schultz, 'Provocative comments go both ways, prime minister', Crikey, 14 November 2019, www.crikey.com.au/2019/11/14/provocative-statements-scott-morrison.

8   Settlement, conquest or something else?

1   *Coe v Commonwealth* (1979) 53 *ALJR* 403. Although, as outlined in chapter 5, this judgment denied Coe's claim of sovereignty, Justice Murphy did state, 'The plaintiff is entitled to endeavour to prove that the concept of terra nullius had no application to Australia, that the lands were acquired by conquest, and to rely upon the legal consequences which follow'.

2   A Colonist, 'Original correspondence: market commission', *Port Phillip Gazette*, 28 May 1842.

3   'Gentleman in New South Wales' to Methodist Missionary Society, In Correspondence: Australia, 1812–26, AJCP, FM4, 1398-1421.

4   Robinson to Whitcomb, 10 August 1832, George Augustus Robinson Papers, ML, A 7022–7092, vol. 14.

5   GC Mundy, *Our Antipodes*, 3 vols, Richard Bentley, London, 1852, vol. 1, p. 226.

6   T Bartlett, *New Holland*, Longman, Brown, Green, and Longmans, London, 1843, p. 78.

7   'The Blacks', *Moreton Bay Courier*, 16 January 1847.

8   'The "children of the soil"', *Moreton Bay Courier*, 9 December 1848.

9   E Landor, *The Bushman, or Life in a New Country*, Richard Bentley, London, 1847, pp. 187–88. Original italics.

10   Senate Standing Committee on Constitutional and Legal Affairs, *Two Hundred Years Later*, Report on the feasibility of a compact or 'Makarrata' between the Commonwealth and Aboriginal people, AGPS, Canberra, 1983, pp. 45–46.

11   YZ Blum, *Historic Titles in International Law*, Nijhoff, The Hague, 1965, pp. 99–100.

12   R Phillimore, *Commentaries upon International Law*, 4 vols, T & JW Johnson, Philadelphia, 1854, vol. 1, pp. 216, 217.

13   See chapter 4, note 8.

14   WE Hall, *A Treatise on the Foreign Powers and Jurisdiction of the British Crown*, Clarendon Press, London, 1894, p. 224.

15   Hall, *A Treatise on the Foreign Powers*, p. 228.

9   The cost of conquest

1   H Reynolds, *This Whispering in Our Hearts*, Allen & Unwin, Sydney, 1998. Revised and republished as *This Whispering in Our Hearts Revisited*, NewSouth, Sydney, 2018.

2   Djon Mundine, *The Aboriginal Memorial*, National Gallery of Australia, nga.gov.au/aboriginalmemorial/history.cfm.

3   E Curr, *The Australian Race*, vol 1, pp. 100–101, 209.

4   Stanner, *After the Dreaming*, p. 25.

5   WEH Stanner, 'The Aborigines', in JCG Kevin (ed.), *Some Australians Take Stock*, Longmans, Green & Co., London, 1939, p. 8.

6   W Murdoch, *The Making of Australia*, Whitcomb & Tombs, Melbourne, 1917, p. 9.

7   WK Hancock, *Australia*, 2nd edn, Australasian Publishing Co., Sydney, 1945, pp. 29–30.

8   JA La Nauze, 'The study of Australian history, 1929–1959', *Historical Studies*, vol. 9, no. 33, 1959, p. 11.

9   JM Ward, *Empire in the Antipodes: The British in Australasia 1840–1860*, Arnold, London, 1966, p. 50.

10   R Ward, *Australia*, Horwitz, Sydney, 1965, p. 11.

11   D Pike *Australia: The Quiet Continent*, CUP, Cambridge, 1962.

12   R Ward, *Australia*, p. 27; KS Inglis, 'Mark Twain and the Gilded Age', *Australian Economic History Review*, vol. 7, no. 1, 1967, pp. 19–37.

13   Anon., *The Queen of the Colonies; or, Queensland as I Knew it*, Sampson Low, London, 1876, p. 340.

14   B Spencer & FJ Gillen, *Across Australia*, 2 vols, Macmillan, London, 1912, vol. 1, p. 189.

15   P Hasluck, *Black Australians*, MUP, Melbourne, 1942, p. 13.

16   M Barnard, *A History of Australia*, Angus & Robertson, Sydney, 1963, p. 653.

17   JB Cleland, 'The future of the Australian Aboriginal', *Medical Journal of Australia*, vol. 47, no. 1, 1960, p. 29.

18   *The Way We Civilize*, G & J Black, Brisbane, 1880.

19   H Reynolds, 'Violence: the Aboriginals, and the Australian historian', *Meanjin*, vol. 31, no. 4, December 1972, pp. 471–77.

20   H Reynolds (ed.), *Race Relations in North Queensland*, JCU, Townsville, 1978, pp. 24, 50.

21   H Reynolds, *The Other Side of the Frontier*, JCU, Townsville, 1981, p. 99.

22   See M Finnane, 'Just like a "nun's picnic"? Violence and colonisation in Australia', *Current Issues in Criminal Justice*, vol. 14, no. 3, 2003, pp. 299–305.

23   See R Manne (ed.), *Whitewash: On Keith Windschuttle's Fabrication of Aboriginal History*, Black Inc., Melbourne, 2003.

24   See I McFarlane, *Beyond Awakening: The Aboriginal Tribes of North-West Tasmania*, Fullers, Launceston, 2008; G Calder Levee, *Line and Martial Law*, Fullers, Launceston, 2010; N Clements, *The Black War*, UQP, Brisbane, 2014.

25   See T Roberts, *Frontier Justice: A History of the Gulf Country to 1900*, UQP, Brisbane, 2005; and C Owen, *Every Mother's Son is Guilty: Policing the Kimberley Frontier 1882–1905*, UWAP, Perth, 2016.

26   J Richards, *The Secret War: A True History of Queensland's Native Police*, UQP, Brisbane, 2008; T Bottoms, *Conspiracy of Silence: Queensland's Frontier Killing Times*, Allen & Unwin, Sydney, 2013; R Ørsted-Jensen, *Frontier History Revisited*, Lux Mundi, Brisbane, 2011.

10   Queensland was different

1   Grey to Fitzroy, 10 February 1850, Colonial Office, CO/208/58, UK National Archives.

2   *Queensland Guardian*, 22 July 1861.

3   *QPD*, 21 October 1880, vol. 32, pp. 1130–35.

4   Palmer to Howitt, 5 August 1882, AW Howitt Papers, MS 9356, box 5, folder 1, La Trobe Collection, SLV.

5   R Evans & Robert Ørsted-Jensen, '"I cannot say the numbers that were killed": assessing violent mortality on the Queensland frontier', SSRN, 19 July 2004, papers.ssrn.com/sol3/papers.cfm?abstract_id=2467836, p. 4. See also J Richards, *Secret War: A True History of Queensland's Native Police*, UQP, Brisbane, 2008.

6   Evans & Ørsted-Jensen, '"I cannot say the numbers that were killed"', p. 5.

7   Evans & Ørsted-Jensen, '"I cannot say the numbers that were killed"', p. 6.

8   *Queensland Guardian*, 4 May 1861.

9   'A new way with the northern blacks', *The Queenslander*, 15 February 1879.

10   Select Committee on the Native Police, *Queensland Votes & Proceedings*, 1861, p. 9a.

11   'Native Police incidents III: reminiscences of the early sixties by an ex-officer', *The Queenslander*, 17 June 1899.

12   *Rockhampton Bulletin*, 8 November 1870.

13   'The Native Police', *The Queenslander*, 8 March 1879.

14   'The blacks and the selector', *The Queenslander*, 26 November 1887.

15   C Atfield, 'Australian War Memorial should recognise revised Aboriginal death toll: researcher', *Brisbane Times*, 16 July 2014, www.brisbanetimes.com.au/national/queensland/australian-war-memorial-should-recognise-revised-aboriginal-death-toll-researcher-20140716-ztqr6.html.

16   'Shall we admit the blacks?', *Port Denison Times*, 1 May 1869.

11   Remembering the dead

1   CJM Scallon, 'Aboriginee [sic] hereditary ingratitude', *Science of Man*, vol. 4, no. 7, 21 August 1901, p. 115.

2   R Howitt, *Australia: Historical, Descriptive, and Statistic*, Longman, Brown, Green, and Longmans, London, 1845, p. 276.

3   F Dutton, *South Australia and its Mines*, T and W Boone, London, 1845, p. 323.

4   *Rockhampton Bulletin*, 28 August 1865.

5   Richards, *The Secret War*, p. 220.

6   'The natives in the far north III', *Sydney Morning Herald*, 23 August 1880.

7   RJ Scholl, quoted in P Hasluck, *Black Australians*, p. 171.

8   *Hodgkinson Mining News*, 29 December 1877.

9   E Eyre, *Journals of Expeditions of Discovery*, vol. 2, pp. 216–17.

10 J.E., 'The Aborigines', *Launceston Advertiser*, 26 September 1831.

11 K Inglis, *Sacred Places: War Memorials in the Australian Landscape*, Miegunyah Press, Melbourne, 1998, p. 471.

12 See, for example, 'Media Release – Australian War Memorial unveils "The Soul of the Nation" experience', 8 April 2019, VeteransSA, veteranssa.sa.gov. au/2019/04/media-release-australian-war-memorial-unveils-the-soul-of-the-nation-experience.

13 Quoted in S Wareham, 'AWM Redevelopment', John Menadue – Pearls and Irritations (blog), 11 November 2019, johnmenadue.com/sue-wareham-awm-redevelopment-green-lights-all-the-way-despite-widespread-opposition.

12   The consequences of truth-telling

1   S Levin, 'Lynching memorial leaves some quietly seething: "Let sleeping dogs lie"', *The Guardian*, 28 April 2018, www.theguardian.com/us-news/2018/apr/28/lynching-memorial-backlash-montgomery-alabama.

2   J Fermoso, 'A 124-year-old statue reviled by Native Americans – and how it came down', *The Guardian*, 24 September 2018, www.theguardian.com/us-news/2018/sep/24/early-days-statue-removed-san-francisco-native-americans.

3   A Mohdin, R Adams & B Quinn, 'Oxford college backs removal of Cecil Rhodes statue', 18 June 2020, *The Guardian*, www.theguardian.com/education/2020/jun/17/end-of-the-rhodes-cecil-oxford-college-ditches-controversial-statue.

4   D Olusoga, 'Why are so many afraid to confront Britain's historical links with the slave trade?', *The Guardian*, 5 May 2019, www.theguardian.com/commentisfree/2019/may/05/why-are-so-many-afraid-to-confront-britains-links-with-the-slave-trade.

5   S Carrell, 'Glasgow University to pay £20m in slave trade reparations', *The Guardian*, 23 August 2019, www.theguardian.com/uk-news/2019/aug/23/glasgow-university-slave-trade-reparations.

6   'Edward Colston statue: Protesters tear down slave trader monument', BBC News, 8 June 2020, www.bbc.com/news/uk-52954305; 'Robert Milligan: slave trader statue removed from outside London museum', BBC News, 9 June 2020, www.bbc.com/news/uk-england-london-52977088.

7   BA Allen et al., *Slavery and Justice: Report of the Brown University Steering Committee on Slavery and Justice*, Brown University, Providence, Rhode Island, n.d. (2006), brown.edu/Research/Slavery_Justice/documents/SlaveryAndJustice.pdf.

8   C Knaus, '"No pride in genocide": vandals deface Captain Cook statue in Sydney's Hyde park', *The Guardian*, 26 August 2017, www.theguardian.com/australia-news/2017/aug/26/captain-cook-statue-and-two-others-in-sydneys-hyde-park-attacked-by-vandals.

9   D Kozaki, 'NSW government to consider tightening laws after second Captain Cook statue vandalised', ABC News, 15 June 2020, www.abc.net.au/news/2020-06-15/second-captain-cook-statue-vandalised-in-sydney/12354896.

10   B Scates, 'Monumental errors: how Australia can fix its racist colonial statues', *The Conversation*, 28 August 2017, theconversation.com/monumental-errors-how-australia-can-fix-its-racist-colonial-statues-82980.

11   Scates, 'Monumental errors.

12   'Government resident's report on Northern Territory for the year 1887', *SAPP*, vol. 3, no. 17, 1888; see aiatsis.gov.au/sites/default/files/docs/digitised_collections/remove/58809.pdf.

13   C Owen, *'Every Mother's Son is Guilty': Policing the Kimberley Frontier of Western Australia 1881–1905*, UWA Press, Perth, 2016, p. 359.

14   T Roberts, 'The brutal truth: what happened in the Gulf Country', *The Monthly*, November 2009, p. 5, www.themonthly.com.au/issue/2009/november/1330478364/tony-roberts/brutal-truth.

15   See A Nettelbeck & R Foster, *In the Name of the Law*, Wakefield Press, Adelaide, 2007.

16   *Mabo v Queensland (No. 2)* (1992) 175 *CLR* 1, at p. 80.

13   Inescapable iconoclasm
1   *Griffith Review*, no. 60, *First Things First*, p. i.
2   *QPD*, vol. 33, 13 September 1880, p. 675.
3   NA Loos, *Invasion and Resistance*, ANU Press, Canberra, 1982, pp. 103–109.
4   'Princeton will remove Woodrow Wilson's name from school', *New York Times*, 27 June 2020, www.nytimes.com/2020/06/27/nyregion/princeton-university-woodrow-wilson.html.

Conclusion: The resurgent north
1   'The Uluru Statement from the Heart', ulurustatement.org/the-statement.
2   'Native title', Australian Trade and Investment Commission, www.austrade.gov.au/land-tenure/Native-title/native-title.
3   'Native title overview', Kimberley Land Council, www.klc.org.au/native-title-overview.
4   N Peterson & F Myers (eds), *Experiments in Self Determination: Histories of the Outstation Movement in Australia*, ANU Press, Canberra, 2016, p. 14; 'Aboriginal homelands & outstations', Creative Spirits, www.creativespirits.info/aboriginalculture/land/aboriginal-homelands-outstations.

INDEX

Index

Index

Index